The Stacked Deck and the Myth of Sovereignty

The Illegality of the Dispossession of Australia's First Nations People

Louis A Coutts

BALBOA.PRESS

A DIVISION OF HAY HOUSE

Balboa Press books may be ordered through booksellers or by contacting:

Balboa Press
A Division of Hay House
1663 Liberty Drive
Bloomington, IN 47403
www.balboapress.com.au
AU TFN: 1 800 844 925 (Toll Free inside Australia)
AU Local: (02) 8310 7086 (+61 2 8310 7086 from outside Australia)

Print information available on the last page.

ISBN: 978-1-9822-9717-6 (sc)
ISBN: 978-1-9822-9718-3 (e)

Balboa Press rev. date: 05/29/2023

Contents

1

Introduction

In my declining years of retirement, my interest in the law has not abated, and so it was that recently I revisited the first definitive book on Australian constitutional law by the then-eminent lawyers Quick and Garren, who were involved in the debates leading up to the adoption of the Constitution and were responsible for most of its drafting. The first part of the book is historical and traverses the history of the establishment of British institutions throughout its extraordinary empire. It is unrestrained in its praise of the wonderful achievement of the British establishment in spreading the benefits of its principles of government and law that had bestowed such wonderful privileges on those who occupied its vast domain. Its history of Australia commences in 1770, when Captain Cook proclaimed possession of and sovereignty over this country on behalf of George III and laid the foundation for the beneficence of English law to guide the destiny of this new territory as though nothing existed before 1770. There is one mention in this introduction to the possibility of some preceding enterprise by referring to people living in the country at the time of the arrival of the First Fleet as "savages."

The book then goes on to describe the debates about the important issues involved in bringing all the colonies together in one federation without any mention of the "savages." And when the debates were over and the dust settled on the draft of our Constitution, there were but two mentions of the savages in that document. One denied the new Parliament the power to make laws in relation to the Aboriginal population of the country. The other provided that the population of the Aborigines should not be taken into account in calculating the population of this country. These were not accidental provisions but fundamentally necessary to justify the myth that sovereignty passed to the Crown in 1770. According to the law as it was developed by the Privy Council in the previous century, this land was unoccupied at the time of the arrival of Captain Cook other than by barbarians or savages.

In its unqualified praise for the wonderful enterprise of British colonisation, no mention is made of its underpinning by the slave trade, of the exportation of convicts to provide free labour to the new domains. No mention is made of the violence by which it took possession of many of its jewels. No mention is made of the outrageous operation of the notorious East India Company in conducting the largest and most oppressive protection racket in history or of the rape of Africa by Cecil Rhodes and his mates. In 1900 the authors reflected on the wonderful benefits that the monarchical English establishment brought to this country without mentioning that one of the benefits was the subjection of the indigenous people to British law, resulting in their imprisonment, shackling in irons, and hangings, not to mention their removal from their sacred lands.

As I was reading this stuff, the lawyer in me became troubled. How could a simple planting of flags and a proclamation by a sailor mysteriously transfer from the hundreds of thousands of people who inhabited this island total control over their destinies to a monarch of whom they had never heard and without their consent?

All my life, and particularly that period of life as a lawyer, I had always accepted unquestionably the robustness of our legal underpinnings. I suppose everyone has their light-bulb moments, but at this late stage of my life, I had mine. By what miracle did words written by a sailor, albeit an outstanding sailor, vest this crown of jewels we call Australia in the hands of the Crown in England? The law expects that events of such moment are painfully negotiated and involve the consent of both parties. But here, in assuming sovereignty over this land, there was no participation of the inhabitants in this massive transfer of their entitlements and the surrender of their laws and customs to the newcomers.

With nothing better to do with my time, I spent an inordinate amount of time in the Melbourne University Law Library to explore this legal miracle. I was shocked at what I discovered. In 1770, according to both English common law and international law, sovereignty could only legally be acquired over unoccupied territory. For over two hundred years, the uninformed Law Lords on the Privy Council, which was the highest judicial authority in the empire, persisted with the myth that this country was unoccupied because the inhabitants were barbarian or savages. The fact that the opposite was the case became part of the finding in a decision in a major case by a justice of the Supreme Court of the Northern Territory in 1971. It was finally accepted officially that in 1788, this land had been occupied over tens of thousands of years by a highly civilised people. In 1770 and in 1788, this country was not terra nullius.

The indigenous people were quick to set the record straight and applied to the court for a finding that sovereignty never passed to the Crown in 1770. If this land was occupied by the original inhabitants at the time of Captain Cook's proclamation, sovereignty could not have passed to the Crown. On the face of it, that was a pretty powerful argument, but the High Court put an end to it in one sentence. Judge Gibbs said, "You cannot argue that issue in our Courts."

After months of research, I came to the conclusion that Gibbs was wrong, and there is no impediment to the indigenous people challenging the validity of sovereignty in our courts, and if they were permitted to do so, they would be able to establish that sovereignty never legally passed to the Crown.

There is a current buzz of excitement that we are going to have a referendum to set the record straight. Based on the history of failed referendums in this country, I wouldn't hold my breath about the outcome.

On the other hand, if the judges of the High Court had their feet held to the fire and declared that sovereignty did not pass to the Crown in 1770, there would be no need for a referendum.

Following is the sad story of ignorance, condescension, and arrogance at the highest levels of the judicial system over the past two hundred years that have kept the indigenous people in their place.

2

The High Court of Australia

In order to understand the circumstances leading up to the denial of the right of the descendants of the original inhabitants of this county to challenge the legality of the original proclamation of sovereignty over their country, it is necessary to understand something of our High Court. The High Court was established according to our Constitution to be the highest court in the land and the final court of appeal from the country's lower courts. It has a maximum membership of seven, but it is not unusual for fewer judges to hear and determine a case, sometimes with disastrous results when an even number of judges are divided in their opinions.

There is a belief in the wider community that the High Court, made up of the leading lawyers in the country, is infallible. The opposite is, in fact, the case. The extent of disagreement between the judges of the High Court is legendary. Judges of the High Court and the lower courts in this country are constrained in their decision-making by the doctrine of what the lawyers call "precedent." If a case comes before a court and it is found that there have been similar cases in the past where a higher court had ruled on the same issue, lower courts are bound by that decision irrespective of whether it was fair or just. The High Court is not bound to follow decisions of any other court in the world, yet its judges trawl the legal archives of the world for opinions of different judges in different parts of the world for guidance.

It would be comforting if all this learning, together with the doctrine of precedent, lent itself to certainty in the law, but that is far from the truth of the matter. All this plethora of learning does is to confuse, resulting in different judges coming to decisions diametrically opposite those of their fellow judges on the same set of facts. Sometimes a virus infects the law as a result of an erroneous decision of some superior court in the distant past, but this erroneous principle is still relied on as a precedent. Sadly, this has been the case in major indigenous cases that have come before the High Court. But before we visit those cases, it is worthwhile mentioning some decisions of the court that demonstrate the extent of disagreement between its judges and the uncertainty about the law that exists at the highest level of our judicial system.

In 1996, a woman was apprehended by the police in Liverpool and her handbag searched. A spray irritant was discovered, and she was prosecuted for carrying the irritant without a reasonable excuse. Her excuse was that she had previously been attacked by a man and carried the irritant to defend herself in the event of a subsequent attack. Three judges held that she didn't have a reasonable excuse, two said she did, and on the vote of one, her conviction stood.

Two young girls were sexually assaulted by their teacher in a one-teacher school in Queensland Country. They sued the education department on the basis that it owed them a duty of care not to be molested by their teacher. A majority of judges held that the department was not liable because the teacher acted criminally, and they had not employed him to act criminally. A minority held that the department was clearly liable to ensure that children in their care were not molested or mistreated.

There was the case in which the court was divided over the issue of whether the Swan River was a river or the sea. A majority said it was the sea; a minority said it was a river.

In another case, it took all the judges to deliver a separate judgement to decide that the words, "any other person," meant, "any other person."

In 2004, a question came before the court as to whether in 1963 a principle of law mentioned in a textbook in 1674 that said a husband had immunity from prosecution for raping his wife was still good law. Three said it wasn't, and two said it was.

A case of major constitutional importance questioned whether the state of New South Wales could retain one billion dollars paid to it by the tobacco industry or if it should go to the Commonwealth. Three said the Commonwealth should get the money, and two said the state should keep it. On the vote of one, the state lost a billion dollars.

Then in another major constitutional case, there was an appeal from a decision of the federal court (a decision which I thought was clearly wrong). It was of such importance that the states sent a team of high-priced barristers to Canberra to argue the case. Only six judges heard the case, and three judges in two decisions agreed with the federal court, and three judges in separate decisions disagreed, resulting in a three-all draw; the decision of the lower court stood. Over the next twelve months, there was a change in the personnel of the High Court when the issue was once again argued, and on that occasion, with one exception, the new judges overturned the decision of the federal court.

Sometimes the stakes are extremely high as they were for a guy convicted of manslaughter and sentenced to thirteen years in prison. He appealed to the Queensland Court of Appeal, and the three judges unanimously decided he should be acquitted. The Crown appealed to the High Court. Three judges decided he should be imprisoned for thirteen years, and two decided that he shouldn't.

These cases prompted me to embark on a study of four hundred consecutively reported decisions of the court over a ten-year period in order to get a more accurate picture of the reliability of our High Court in particular and our legal system in general. How effective is this doctrine of precedent? I discovered that there were dissenting judgements in over 50 per cent of those cases. A dissenting judgement is one diametrically opposed to the opinions of the majority. In only a small percentage of cases were unanimous decisions given, and in most cases where all judges came to the same conclusion, they did so by delivering separate judgements.

One alarming statistic that stood out as a challenge to the effectiveness of the doctrine of precedent was the percentage of successful appeals from the Federal Court of Appeal to the High Court. During the period of my review, over 60 per cent of appeals from the decision of the Federal Court of Appeal were successful. This means that either the judges on the Federal Court of Appeal got it wrong 60 per cent of the time or the High Court or both.

This review convinced me that the doctrine of precedent was not working. One problem seemed to be that courts were dealing with new social phenomena while relying on decisions made in previous eras.

But can I come back to indigenous issues that have only been illuminated in relatively recent time? When I started reading the book by Quick and Garren mentioned in the introduction, I was struck by the incongruity of a legal principle that sovereignty over people and ownership of their land could be acquired without their consent, not to mention these people becoming subject to the laws of an unknown monarch. I wondered the extent to which the failure of the doctrine of precedent enabled our High Court to legitimise sovereignty and the dispossession. The following chapters are the story of my journey, and I was saddened by my discoveries.

Indigenous issues have a sixty thousand–year history, but it is only in the last seventy or eighty years that archaeologists and anthropologists captured attention, and together with the indigenous people, have shone an ever-increasingly sharp light on the spiritual and religious depths of these ancient people. It saddened me that this extraordinary heritage has been the plaything of our legal system.

But one thing is so clear to me: Despite the ancient life of the Aboriginal civilisation, it is now a contemporary issue of profound importance to the future of this country, and to submit this issue to the language of arrogant, uninformed, and condescending judges who sat on the Privy Council in the eighteenth and nineteenth centuries is nothing short of insulting.

It was to the High Court that the indigenous people sought relief in a number of important cases to which the court more often than not turned a deaf ear. Two of the decisions that reflect a deep-seated belief in the traditions of our English legal system at the expense of the interest of the indigenous people were the refusal to allow them to challenge sovereignty in our courts and the rejection of the claim of the stolen generation. But there were others, and we visit them in the next chapters.

One of the difficulties with our legal system is that it is based upon precedent, which means that when contemporary issues such as indigenous issues come before the court, the courts are looking to the past for guidance. It is like driving a car by looking in the rear-view mirror, sometimes with dumbfounding results. For instance, I mentioned the case where three judges mercifully made the decision that a principle of law exculpating a husband from a charge of wife rape dating from 1674 was no longer law in 1963. Nevertheless, two judges decided that it was still good law in 1963 in Australia.

Let us now look at how the British legal system, and more recently the High Court, met the challenge of the emerging discoveries of the true status of this country's indigenous people as representing the descendants of the original inhabitants, who had developed a civilisation that had preserved the beauty of this country for over forty thousand years.

3

The Myth of Terra Nullius

By 1969, a combination of events emboldened the Yolngu people of the Northern Territory to seek the protection of our legal system against nearly two centuries of devastating destruction of the ageless civilisation that had lived in harmony with the sacred land of this untroubled country. Hitherto, the indigenous people only troubled our courts when brought before them for offending our laws. These encounters were often stepping stones to our prison system, which wrought havoc to individuals and carnage to their ancient culture. Sadly, our court system and particularly the High Court, beset with its uncertainty, divisiveness, and reliance on the frequently uninformed decisions of past eras, was unqualified to respond to the indigenous challenge to the legality of the dispossession of their land by the newcomers. The challenge of the Yolngu people in 1969 was not only to navigate the uncertain waters of the Australian legal system but to turn the tide of legal thinking that, for centuries, had relegated the indigenous people of the British Empire to the status of barbarians.

Before we visit the fate of the Yolngu people's 1969 case, it is important to visit the precedents that existed in English and international law at the time of the arrival of the First Fleet.

A couple years before Captain Cook planted the English flag in Botany Bay and proclaimed the land on behalf of the king, the Swiss lawyer Emer de Vattel published a book on international law that still has credence today. It was written at the time of voyages of discovery that, of course, raised issues of the legality of taking possession of foreign lands.

According to Vattel, the law in this regard had its origins in what he called "the law of nature." According to the law of nature, occupiers of nations had to find their sustenance in nature, and the land was the source of that sustenance. As the human population grew, so did the requirement for land. As the requirement for land exceeded the land available to people in a nation, it became the duty of those people, according to the law of nature, to find new pastures. Otherwise, land that was capable of supporting more people would go to waste. The pursuit of these new pastures gave rise to the opportunity for people to extend sovereignty over newly discovered lands. This is how Vattel put it as recorded in the 1792 English-language edition (the original edition was published in 1758):

> All mankind have an equal right to the things that have not fallen into the possession of anyone; and these things belong to the first possessor. When therefor a nation finds a country uninhabited and without a master, it may lawfully take possession of it: and after it has sufficiently made known its will in this respect, it cannot be deprived of it by another.

> Thus navigators going on the discovery, furnished with a commission of their

> sovereign, and meeting with islands, or other desert countries have taken possession of them in the name of their nation; and this title has been commonly respected, provided it was soon after followed by a real possession …

> The law of nations then only recognises the property and sovereignty of a nation over uninhabited countries, of which they shall really and in fact take possession, in which they shall form settlements, or of which they shall make actual use.[1]

Vattel makes the point that the taking possession of the land can only be lawful when, "a nation finds a country uninhabited and without a master." At this point in time, 1792, the taking possession of this country by the Crown wouldn't stand the test of legality as outlined by Vattel. The country was inhabited to the knowledge of the newcomers and their masters in England.

Almost simultaneously with the publication of Vattel's treaty, Sir William Blackstone published a monumental document that has become known as *Sir William Blackstone's Commentaries* in which he catalogued much of English common law. His mind also turned to the legal issues arising

---

[1] Emer de Vattel, *The Law of Nations: or, Principles of the Law of Nature; Applied to the Conduct and Affairs of Nations and Sovereigns. A Work Tending to Display the True Interest of Powers* (Dublin: Luke White, 1792), p. 164. Translated from the French.

out of the voyages of discovery. This is what he had to say in 1765:

> So long as it was confined to the stocking and cultivation of desert uninhabited countries, it kept strictly within the limits of the law of nature. But how far the seizing on countries already peopled, and driving out or massacring the innocent and defenceless natives, merely because they differed from their invaders in language, in religion, in customs, in government, or in colour; how far such a conduct was consonant to nature, to reason, or to Christianity, deserved well to be considered by those, who have rendered their names immortal by thus civilizing mankind.[2]

Perhaps you can see the problem confronting the lawyers in relation to Britain taking possession of foreign lands. Everyone knew that this new land discovered by Captain Cook was occupied by the natives. So how did the newcomers get around the precedent of both international and English common law? A simple exercise in what might be called legal algebra highlights the issue.

As of 1788, international and English common law were congruent in that it was provided that a foreign sovereign could not proclaim sovereignty over newly discovered lands if they were occupied. By 1992, the High Court accepted that in 1788, this land was in fact occupied by the indigenous

---

[2] *Sir William Blackstone's Commentaries.*

people. These two factors in the equation must equal the factor that we can call illegality. Exercising sovereignty over an occupied territory was illegal according to international and English common law.

And yet, over the two centuries since 1788, the indigenous people were dispossessed of their land. Ownership of their land passed to the newcomers, and they became subject to the laws of the Crown. How could this happen? The story is a sad one of the rape of Anglo/Australian jurisprudence by members of a British institution called the Privy Council, which was the final court of appeal from lower courts throughout the British Empire. The Privy Council created and gave legal credulity to the myth that despite all the evidence to the contrary, Australia was unoccupied.

In 1788, the inhabitants of this country had absolutely no idea how they and their land were perceived by the newcomers. Indeed, nearly a century passed before many of the indigenous people even knew of the arrival of the British. The fact that according to English law they had lost their sovereignty to a new monarch thirteen thousand miles away was completely unknown to them. They had their own laws, their own ways of settling disputes—some peaceful and some violent—since time immemorial. But they had no conception of the new legal system that had descended upon them and their land. It was not until 1992 that two judges of the High Court had the courage to summarise their sad history:

> An early flash point with one clan of
> Aborigines illustrates the first stages of the
> conflagration of oppression and conflict

which was, over the following century, to spread across the continent to dispossess, degrade and devastate the Aboriginal people and leave a national legacy of unutterable shame.[3]

For nearly two hundred years, the British and Australian judicial system had consistently adjudicated issues that directly affected the indigenous people without them ever having seen the inside of the courts in which their fates were being decided, let alone having a say in their outcomes.

In 1847 in New South Wales, a dispute arose between a citizen of that state and the attorney general over the question of title to a certain parcel of land. The issue was the appropriate law to apply in the circumstances. Mr Chief Justice Stephens, who had emigrated to Van Diemen's land some years earlier with some legal qualifications and had risen to the position of chief justice of the Supreme Court of New South Wales, had this to say:

> The Territory of New South Wales, and eventually, the whole island of which it forms a part, have been taken possession of by British subjects in the name of the Sovereign. They belong therefore to the British Crown … The fact of the settlement of New South Wales in that manner and that it forms part of the Queen's Dominions and is subject to and governed by British law may be learned from public colonial

---

[3] Mabo v. Queensland 1992 CLR 1 at page 104.

> records and from Acts of Parliament. New
> South Wales is termed in the Statute 54
> George III c15 and in 59 George III c 122,
> His Majesty's colony, not even the colony of
> the Empire … that the waste lands of this
> colony are, and ever have been, from the time
> of its first settlement in 1788, in the Crown,
> that they are and ever have been from that
> date (in point of legal intendment), without
> office found, in the Sovereign's possession,
> and that, as his or her property, they have
> been and may now be effectively granted to
> subjects of the Crown.[4]

Looking at this statement today, it is challenging to think that the simple act of placing a flag in the ground and the printing of a document and its reading in Sydney Cove in 1788 deprived the then-inhabitants of their association with the land they had cared for, for tens of thousands of years, and rendered them and the land subject to the laws of the English monarch. And this without them having any knowledge of what was going on. This definitive statement—that the laws of England became the laws of New South Wales in 1788 and that the land of this vast country became the possession of King George III—was surprising given that an informed lawyer in 1847 would be familiar with the writings of the distinguished lawyers Emer de Vattel and Sir William Blackstone.

There were many occasions over the 180 years following the arrival of the First Fleet for the courts to consider the

---

[4] Brown v. Attorney General of New South Wales, 1847.

status of the natives of different territories that formed the British Empire. In this period of legal history, as white settlement expanded throughout the colony of New South Wales, it was impossible to avoid the observation that the land was in fact occupied by indigenous people. On the face of it, forcing them from their historic association with the land was against the natural law according to Vattel, and against the laws of England according to Blackstone. This little difficulty was easily overcome by the English judicial enterprise. There was an implicit recognition that the natives were in fact present in the various domains of this country, but their presence had to be dismissed as people "occupying" the land for fear that a recognition of any natural rights to the land would trigger the principles of Vattel and Blackstone.

These are some examples of how the courts dealt with this tricky situation. For example, in 1863 Lord Kingsdown, sitting on the Privy Council, made this pronouncement:

> Where Englishmen establish themselves
> in an uninhabited or barbarous country,
> they carry with them, not only the laws
> but the sovereignty of their own state and
> those who live amongst them and become
> members of their community become also
> partakers of and subject to the same laws.[5]

So the word "uninhabited" crept into the lexicon of the law as it applied to newly acquired territories of the Crown.

---

[5] Advocate-General of Bengal v. Ranee Surnomoye Dossee (48) (1863) 2 Moo N S 22, at p. 59 [1863] EngR 761; 15 ER 811, at p. 824.

Gradually, this term became known as terra nullius, which is roughly translated from the Latin by lawyers as "land unoccupied." Lord Kingsdown was really saying that despite their presence in the new domains of the Crown, the inhabitants were barbarous, and therefore, the country was uninhabited.

In 1888, a dispute between two citizens of New South Wales reached the Privy Council, giving rise to the necessity for their lordships to pronounce on the legal status of New South Wales. Lord Watson used the following language:

> The extent to which British law is introduced into a British colony, and the manner of its introduction, must necessarily vary according to circumstances. There is a great difference between a Colony acquired by conquest or cession, in which there is an established system of law, and that of a Colony which consisted of a tract of territory practically unoccupied, without settled inhabitants or settled law, at the time when it was peacefully annexed to the British Dominions. The Colony of New South Wales belongs to the latter class.[6]

The condescending language used by members of the Privy Council to justify the disinheritance of the natives of the far-flung British Empire continued well into the twentieth century. For example, in a case where Cecil Rhodes sought

______

[6] Cooper v. Stuart (1889), 14 App Cas, at p. 291.

the imprimatur of the Privy Council to his theft of Southern Rhodesia, this is what Lord Sumner said in 1919:

> The estimation of the rights of aboriginal tribes is always inherently difficult. Some tribes are so low in the scale of social organisation that their usages and conceptions of rights and duties are not to be reconciled with the institutions or legal ideas of a civilised society.[7]

In 1936, Winston Churchill (as he then was), in giving evidence to the Royal Commission into the partitioning of Palestine, said:

> I do not admit, for instance, that a great wrong has been done to the Red Indians of America, or the black people of Australia. I do not admit that a wrong has been done to those people by the fact that a stronger race, a higher-grade race, or, at any rate, a more widely world race, to put it that way, has come in and taken their place. I do not admit it. I do not think that the Red Indians had any right to say, "The American continent belongs to us and we are not going to have any of these European settlers in here." They had not the right nor had they the power.[8]

---

[7] In re Southern Rhodesia (1919), App Cas, 211, at p. 233–234.

[8] See Andrew Roberts, *Churchill; Walking with Destiny* (Penguin Random House, 2018), p. 415.

In a school textbook in the first half of the twentieth century, Walter Murdoch proclaimed that the history of this country is the history of the white people who have lived in Australia. He excluded the Aboriginal people from our history as, "dark skinned wandering tribes who hurled boomerangs and ate snakes."[9]

It was little wonder that our Constitution reflected this view of the Aboriginal people and dismissed them as having no part to play in this country, other than to be treated as criminals if they didn't like our laws. The Aboriginal people are mentioned twice in the Constitution that was adopted in 1901:

> Section 51; The Parliament shall, subject to
> this Constitution, have power to make laws
> for the peace, good order, and Government
> of the Commonwealth with respect to:
>
> > (xxvi) the people of any race, other
> > than the aboriginal race in any state.
>
> Section 127: In reckoning the numbers of
> the people of the Commonwealth or of a
> State or other part of the Commonwealth,
> aboriginal natives shall not be counted.

These clauses were the final legal validations of the dispossession and the assault on indigenous culture. It is the official legal statement that even by 1901, so far as the Aboriginal people were concerned, they didn't exist and

---

[9] See Henry Reynolds, "Introduction," in Henry Reynolds, *Dispossession* (Allen and Unwin, 1989), p. xii.

never had. Accordingly, in 1788, the land was not occupied and was there for the taking on behalf of King George III by a sailor planting a flag in Botany Bay.

It could be asked, "Why was it necessary to include these specific clauses in the Constitution in relation to the Aboriginal people?" The answer is that it was essential to justify the dispossession. If the Aboriginal people didn't exist, or only existed as uncivilised people without laws, then the taking of their land was legal according to both international law and domestic English common law.

Perhaps you can see the problem confronting the lawyers in relation to Britain taking possession of foreign lands. Everyone knew that this new land discovered by Captain Cook was occupied by the natives. So how did the newcomers get around the precedent of both international and domestic law?

The two clauses in the Constitution about the Aboriginal people give us the key. Everyone pretended that the indigenous population didn't exist, and this land was what was called terra nullius. The lawyers overcame this problem by declaring, without any evidence, that the natives were barbaric, uncivilised, and without any system of laws or government, so the land was there for the taking. As we will see, once it became obvious that the Aborigines did exist, the next step was to separate the full-blooded Aborigine from those of mixed blood. The theory was that the full-blooded people would die out, and the others would be assimilated into our society, and the race would disappear, solving many inconvenient legal problems.[10] This fiction persisted for almost two hundred years, during which time over forty thousand years of the history of this country was raped.

In the second half of the last century, some intrepid archaeologists commenced a process of gradually unveiling the curtain that had concealed pre-1788 history for nearly two hundred years. As the story unfolded, it found its way into our judicial system, and after 170 years of dispossession, the indigenous voice was first heard in an Australian court. Before we can evaluate the response of our legal system to the Aboriginal cause, it is necessary to have a little insight into the story as revealed by some of the narratives handed down by the original inhabitants from generation to generation over tens of thousands of years. Archaeological and anthropological discoveries since the middle of the last century are also compelling.

---

[10] See chapter 14, "The Stolen Generation."

4

Pre-1788

To the inhabitants of this country, nothing changed on April 29, 1770. Nor were they aware of any change on January 26, 1788. The rising sun was a passage in the timeless calendar of this vast country, where obligations were not measured by time but by an ageless habit of respect for the ancestral spirits whose existence stretched back to the Dreamtime and the first act of creation of this sacred earth and its people. They were isolated from the catastrophe of European society with its endless wars and inhuman cruelty inflicted upon sinners and non-believers in the name of religion, social inequality that sanctified a hierarchy of indolent people of property dependent on the exploitation of the impoverished, and a reliance on a dysfunctional economy that favoured the already rich at the further expense of the already poor. That is not to diminish some of the sublime moments in European history in the fields of art, literature, and music, but even these became the province of the wealthy. The collision of cultures could not have been more profound when the First Fleet, carrying the overflow of the product of the prison sewers of England, arrived on these shores in 1788. Shortly after their arrival, some of the indigenous people were introduced to the barbaric British practice of unmercifully flogging their own people.

Because European society was structured around and constrained by the inflexibility of time, it developed techniques for recording its activities, resulting in the study of history. It is so easy to visit a Western library and study the history of past ages. Because time meant nothing to the original inhabitants, their history remained undocumented but nevertheless rich in the stories passed down through the ages and the art with which they decorated the rock walls of their habitat.

In this extraordinary state of affairs, an inexplicable phenomenon occurred when Captain Arthur Phillip read his commission from the establishment of King George III in England to the survivors of the eight months' journey in their filthy ships. He completed the process of what became known as an "Act of State," whereby sovereignty over and ownership of the land of this country became vested in King George III. The unsuspecting inhabitants became subject to the laws of His Majesty and surrendered their land to the Crown of England. Thus commenced the continuous major export of England to this country—ignorance and hypocrisy—over the next two hundred years,. Until the second half of the nineteenth century, no attempt was made to unveil the ancient history of this country. And in the meantime, most of its land had been taken from its inhabitants, their population decimated, and their culture, religion, and spirituality ravaged. The continual dispossession of the Aboriginal people in the name of the Crown and with the message of "Christianity" is reminiscent of R. H. Tawney's description of Cromwell's soldier saints:

> While amid the blare of trumpets, and the
> clash of arms, and the rending of the carved

> work of the Temple, humble to God and
> haughty to man, the soldier saints swept
> over the battlefield and scaffold, their
> garments rolled in blood.[11]

The story of the archaeologists and anthropologists who pioneered the tedious task of unveiling the pre-1788 history of this country is told in some splendid detail in the book *Deep Time Dreaming*.[12] In the middle of the last century there was a coincidence of the inquisitiveness of these intrepid pioneers and the refinement of the science known as carbon dating. Rather than the image of the original inhabitants as uncivilised, barbaric, nomadic people without laws or culture, a completely different story emerged. The original inhabitants were the members of an ancient civilisation that had its origins more than forty thousand years earlier. The very process of discovery illuminated the sacredness of this history to the indigenous community. The discovery and disturbance of ancient relics by well-meaning archaeologists was sometimes considered so sacrilegious that the sanctity of ancestral spirits was more important than the revelation of their history.

A significant source of pre-1788 history is contained in narratives of the indigenous people that they have passed down since the period in their history that they identified as the time of creation. While the indigenous people were forced to learn the English language, little effort was made to learn theirs, and either intentionally or deliberately, many

---

[11] R. H. Tawney, *Religion and the Rise of Capitalism* (Version Press, 2015), p. 197. (The book was first published in 1926.)

[12] Billy Griffiths, *Deep Time Dreaming; Uncovering Ancient Australia* (McPherson Publishing Group, 2018; reprinted 2019).

of their languages disappeared. As languages disappeared, the sources of the historical narratives narrowed. But still no serious attempt was made to learn the native languages that would have enlightened the new arrivals to the land with some slight insight into the rich civilisation that had evolved in this country over tens of thousands of years.

As the pre-1788 history of this country emerges, so has the confidence of the indigenous people to proclaim their heritage, resulting in unseemly politicisation and, as we will see, legal ambiguity. One aspect of the politicisation is the attempt by some to equate post-1788 Aboriginal behaviour as a continuation of pre-1788 history with absurd results. The post-1788 disturbance of the Aborigines from their ancient environments resulted in them accommodating poorly to the new Western regime.

It took 180 years before the Aboriginal people first had their voices heard in our judicial system. But before we visit that intersection of ancient custom and English law, it is necessary to have some picture of the civilisation that existed before the arrival of Captain Cook and which became the plaything of the new arrivals. In order to establish a foothold in our legal system, it was essential for the Aboriginal people to establish that this country was not terra nullius, as described in the previous chapter, but occupied by a sophisticated civilisation.

Tucked away in the State Library of Victoria is a collection of papers of the work of the archaeologists and anthropologists in exploring the ancient civilisation of this country and illuminating its richness.[13] One paper is by the anthropologist T. G. H. Strehlow.[14] Mr Strehlow was born on the Hermannsburg mission for the Aboriginal people in Central Australia. One of his mother tongues was that of the Aranda clan, who populated the area.

Strehlow, who grew up with many indigenous people, makes the point that just as there were bad Aborigines, there were bad Europeans, but to represent the conduct of these few as representative of Aboriginal culture and civilisation is as misleading as representing the present-day criminal as typical of modern society. Strehlow tells the story of a people with deep spiritual, religious, and economic relationships with the land that was occupied by their ancestral spirits and which formed the framework of their laws and behaviours. It is the land to which they are intimately related in their lives and to the land they will return so that beyond death, their spirits will be at rest in the land.

Captain Cook made an insightful observation about the Aboriginal people he encountered on his arrival in this country in 1770. Following is an extract from his log:

> From what I have seen of the Natives of
> New Holland, they may appear to some
> as being the most wretched people on
> Earth but in reality they are much more
> happier than we Europeans being wholly
> unacquainted not only with the superfluous
> but the necessary conveniences so much

---

[13] Berndt, R.M and Berndt, C.H., *Aboriginal Man in Australia* (Angus and Robertson, 1965).
[14] Ibid., chapter 5.

> sought after in Europe, they are happy in
> not knowing the use of them.

Missing from this and many subsequent observations by Europeans was any reference to spirituality. All the observations were about their physical appearances and activities. It never occurred to the newcomers that these ancient people might have beliefs about their spirituality and their relationships with each other and the land. The warped view of a vengeful God who punishes sinners in the everlasting fires of hell prevented Europeans from envisaging any other conceivable world view. The fact that the Aboriginal people revealed no such beliefs underpinned the assumption by the white settlers that these naked natives were totally uncivilised.

Mercifully, despite everything, it was not possible to wipe out an ancient civilisation in 150 years, and by 1950, a remnant of the original population still preserved their ancient beliefs. These beliefs had been passed on to succeeding generations over the centuries by way of narratives. Language was so important to these people that they were multilingual and could pass stories across the song lines. Before all these stories disappeared, some have been captured in recent times and translated into our own language. They give a glimpse of a people starkly different from those characterised by the ill-informed members of the Privy Council in the nineteenth and early-twentieth centuries.

A woman by the name of Jean Ellis collected many of these stories and translated them into English and in 2008, had them published.[15] A sample of these stories will provide a little insight into these so called uncivilised people.

The Story of the Unwelcome Owl

This story of "The owl who was unwelcome" comes from the Worona people who lived on the banks of the Fitzroy river.

This is a story of a little boy who discovered an owl that was a bird no one had ever seen before. He told all the other members of his tribe to come and to look at this strange bird. What they didn't realise was that the owl had been sent by their creator, Wandjinu, to find out if there was anything he could do to help these people.

Not knowing this, the young boys grabbed the owl and threw it into the air and let if fall on the ground. They broke one of its wings. Then the adults pulled out its feathers and replaced the feathers with spinifex and plunged the points into the owl's body.

The owl wondered what would become of it when one of the boys once again threw into the air, but instead of falling to the ground, to the surprise of everyone, the owl flew up into the sky and out of site. Wandjinu had

---

[15] Jean Ellis, compiler, *The Dreaming of Aboriginal Australia*, with Aboriginal support. (Penrith Art Printing Works, 2006).

decided to rescue the owl and take it back into the sky. But he also decided to punish the people, except for the few that tried to intervene to stop the torture of the owl.

So Wandjinu ordered the plains to be flooded and one by one the people who had tormented the owl were drowned but those who had tried to save it were dragged by the Kangaroos to safety. The people who were saved by Wandjinu were very caring people and since then have grown into a larger very caring group of people.

I could not help but to reflect on the similarities in this story between the story of the persecution of Christ and the biblical story of the great flood and Noah's ark.

The Golden Boomerang

Now it so happens that Aborigines of the Wiradjuri people believed that the creator was *Byamee* and before Byamee created man and woman he had created the land, the oceans, the rivers and the trees and all the wildlife. The first to be created were the Kangaroo, the Koala, the Eagle and the Emu. These four separately believed that they were better than the others and continually fought amongst themselves.

As their fighting continued, Byamee came down to earth and spoke to them. He suggested that they have a contest to prove which of them was better than the others and invited all the other creatures he had created to come and witness the contest.

When everyone was assembled, the Kangaroo went first and took off and jumped into the sky and over the highest tree and then came back to earth. Everyone thought that the kangaroo was amazing.

Then it was the turn of Eagle who took off and soared out of sight high into the sky and all the animals thought that he must have been lost in the sky but then they saw a small spot in the sky which became bigger and bigger and it turned out to be the Eagle returning. Everyone agreed that that was amazing.

Then came the turn of the Emu who challenged all the other animals to a race. But of course, the Emu was so fast that you could only see a blur and when all the other animals had given up, the Emu was still running.

Finally, the Koala took its turn and climbed up the highest tree and on a flimsy branch, settled itself in and went to sleep. A powerful wind came up and blew at the tree so violently that it was bending but the Koala did not stir and when the wind dropped, it climbed down the tree to Earth.

Byamee congratulated the four and said that he would like to participate. He then took out of his bag a strange instrument which was a crescent shaped piece of wood that he called a boomerang. He then threw the boomerang into the sky and it cleared the tallest tree and went out of site. But then the strangest thing happened. The boomerang reappeared and came down and stopped at Byamee's feet. Everyone was surprised and congratulated Byamee. But he said he wasn't finished. By this time, it was dark and there was no moon. He threw the boomerang back into the sky and this time it didn't come back. Everyone waited and waited and looked into the dark sky when suddenly a bright yellow crescent shape appeared in the sky and from then on, it was never necessary to wait for the full moon for brightness at night.

T. G. H. Strehlow undertook an extraordinary project that involved studying Aboriginal songs and wrote an encyclopaedic volume on the songs of Central Australia,[16] which I discovered in the rare book department of the State Library of Victoria. Following is an extract of a song of women observing nature:

____

[16] T. G. H. Trehlow, *Songs of Central Australia* (Angus and Robertson, 1971).

The Song of the Woman

Among the boulders of the peak we shall
ever sit
A band of sisters we shall ever sit
Among the boulders of the peak we shall
ever sit
Sisters all, let us recline here
From the North the wind is blowing fiercely
From the East the wind is blowing fiercely
The North wind blows incessantly
The East wind blows incessantly
The South wind blows incessantly
The Mountain Hawks scream as they come
swooping down
In the vault of the sky they scream as they
come swooping down
From the vault of the sky they are swooping
down
The Mountain Hawks are swooping down
The Mountain Hawks are descending with
whirring wings
From the vault of the sky they are descending
with whirring wings
They come swooping lower and lower
With hoarse cries they are settling on the
ground

The archaeologist W. E. H. Stanner, in reflecting on the
collision of Western and ancient indigenous civilisation,
commented:

Blindness is an important part of our study. It profoundly affected European conduct towards the Aborigines. It reinforced two opposed views—that they were a survival into modern times of a Proterozoic form of humanity incapable of civilisation, and that they were decadents from a once higher life and culture.[17]

Back in 1840, the lack of understanding of the civilisation that was being progressively destroyed was apparent in a missive from the secretary for colonies sent to Governor Gipps:

> I would submit, therefore, that it is necessary from the moment the Aborigines of this Country are declared British Subjects they should, as far as possible, be taught that the British Laws are to supersede their own, so that any native, who is suffering under their own customs, may have the power of an appeal to those of Great Britain, or, to put this in its true light, that all authorized persons should in all instances be required to protect a native from the violence of his fellows, even though they be in the execution of their own laws.[18]

---

[17] *Religion, Totemism and Symbolism: Aboriginal Man in Australia* (Angus and Robertson, 1965), pp. 208–209.

[18] "Report by Grey on the Method for Promoting the Civilization of Aborigines," enclosure in correspondence, Lord John Russell to Sir George Gipps, October 8, 1840, *HRA* ser. 1, vol. 21, p. 35.

Such was the depth of ignorance of those in England responsible for the colonisation of this country, little aware of the devastation being inflicted on the people who had occupied and cared for this country for ages past.

But stories have survived. The Australian author Robbi Neal travelled to an Aboriginal community on the Cape York Peninsula in 1968 and spent seven years with the community. During that time, she earned the trust of the community, who shared stories of their collision with the British, who removed them from their natural habitat to a mission. The stories are of the transformation of a beautiful people living with and understanding nature; living off the richness of the land to living in compounds and subject to the strict directions of the missionaries and the police, having to wear Western clothes and learn English, forced to abandon their own religion and worship a God who was meaningless to them, and to forsake their Aboriginal names for English names.

Let me quote just one extract from the story of an old woman by the name of Elsie when she first arrived at the mission:

> "This'll teach you lot" said Mr Reverend Rogers. "Beatrice got caught out after dark with that big boy Arnold and Arnold is in jail and Beatrice is on her way there too."
>
> We all stood and watched Beatrice get her hair shaved off and her curls fell to the ground like feathers from a dying bird. Mr Reverend Rogers looked like he'd been waiting a long time to shave off Beatrice's

hair, he looked like nothan in the world could have made him more contented than doing that to Beatrice. And Beatrice cried so hard till she got no more tears left.

"Beatrice and Arnold is marrying age" said my grandmother and she began to wail, frightened that Beatrice would get her liver eaten in the jail and I was frightened too.

"Beatrice and Arnold did propa respect and asked Elders if they are right skin for each other," my father said, coming up an putting his hand on my grandmother's shoulder "and still they go to jail."

My father's face turned dark and from that moment, my father never tickled me or laughed his laugh.[19]

Despite a relatively recent movement to paint a benign picture of the treatment of the Aboriginal people and at the same time recasting their image to sit more comfortably with the nineteenth-century view of the Privy Council, there are lingering and beautiful stories that lend notoriety to that movement.

In 1983, a Doctor W. Peasley, who had an extraordinary background, wrote the story of an Aboriginal man and woman who many years earlier had eloped to escape the dictates of their clan as to whom they should marry. They

---

[19] Robbi Neal, *After before Time* (Harper Collins Australia, 2016), pp. 32–33.

were very much in love and continued to live in the desert even though all the members of the different clans capitulated to urban life. In a drought, it was learnt that this couple were still living in the desert. Dr. Peasley tells the story of their discovery and survival but most of all, of the depth of their love and their intimacy with the land. He called the book *The Last of the Nomads*. Any lawyer contesting the rights of the indigenous people should read the book.[20]

---

[20] W. J. Peasley, *The Last of the Nomads* (Freemantle Press, 1983). There were many reprints until 2009.

5

"Uncivilised" Aboriginal Natives and Our Criminal Law

It was against this background that in 1968, the indigenous people first secured the attention of our judicial system to their plight of dispossession. This involved an application to the Supreme Court of the Northern Territory in what I call the Yolngu people's case. Before I tell you the story of this case, I want to mention two other cases that reached the High Court from the Northern Territory Supreme Court. One preceded the Yolngu people's case by thirty years, and the other was decided thirty years later.

In the earlier case, an Aboriginal man named Tuckiar was charged with murder in the Northern Territory Supreme Court. One of the interesting side issues in this case was that the South Australian criminal law contained a provision that "uncivilised aboriginal natives" could give evidence without taking an oath. In the judgement of the majority of judges of the High Court on appeal, Tuckiar was referred to as an "uncivilised native." Despite being "uncivilised," he was deemed to understand and be subject to English laws.

The facts were as follows.

On August 1, 1933, a police constable named McColl was killed on an island off the coast of Darwin. He and other police had travelled to the island to investigate the recent killings of some Japanese. They came to a deserted native camp on the edge of a thick jungle and found the fires warm. They camped in the vicinity for lunch, posting the trackers round about.

One of the trackers came in with information that enabled the party to surround a number of Aboriginal women. They handcuffed them together and brought them back to camp, where the police questioned them. Later trackers announced that natives were landing in a canoe on a point nearby, and three of the constables and two trackers set off to intercept them. McColl and two trackers were left at the camp with the Aboriginal women, who were at first unfettered.

On the return of the constables, the two trackers were found at the camp, but neither McColl nor the Aboriginal women were there. The next morning, McColl's dead body was found about four hundred yards away from the camp with a spear wound in his chest and a blood-stained spear lying a few paces from it. McColl's pistol showed that he had fired three times, his third shot having been a misfire. Apparently the two trackers, who were left with McColl in charge of the Aboriginal women and were afterwards found at the camp, had not remained there throughout the absence of the rest of the party, who they had probably followed. At any rate, neither of them was called as a witness, and it does not appear why or in what circumstances McColl left the camp.

At the trial, two trackers gave evidence that they had a conversation with Tuckiar in which he admitted the killings. In one, he claimed that Constable McColl fired at him, and he threw a spear at him, killing him. In the other story, he claimed that he saw McColl having sex with one of his Aboriginal women and afterwards, killed him with his spear. In both cases, the stories were consistent with Tuckiar acting in self-defence.

At the trial, just about every principle of evidence designed to protect accused people was abused both by the trial judge and by the counsel for the defence. There were many weaknesses in the Crown's case, and the jury asked the judge what they should do if they were of the opinion that there was insufficient evidence. The judge then gave directions to the jury that could only be interpreted as a direction to convict Tuckiar. One gem of a direction was that as Tuckiar had not given evidence, the jury could interpret that as an admission of guilt. Even in 1934 that was an outrageous statement. The judge also indicated that if the jury acquitted Tuckiar, it could cast aspersions on McColl's character.

What was even worse was that during the trial. when the two trackers had given evidence interpreted in pidgin English, the judge turned to Tuckiar's counsel and said something to the effect that he should speak to his client and ask him which of the accounts was accurate. Counsel foolishly agreed. When he returned, he made a statement that he was in the most difficult situation he had been in, in his professional career.

Tuckiar was convicted and sentenced to death. After the verdict, his counsel stated in open court that Tuckiar had admitted that the evidence of the tracker of his confession of killing the policeman but without mentioning him abusing the Aboriginal women was true. It was all published in the Northern Territory paper. The High Court[21] had no difficulty in upholding the appeal without sparing either the counsel for Tuckiar or the trial judge the harshest criticism.

Tuckiar was released but disappeared while being escorted back to his island by the police. That was what the Northern Territory did to so-called uncivilised aboriginals in those days.

Sixty years later, another Aboriginal person gained access to the High Court in an appeal from the Court of Appeal in the Northern Territory. The problem was that the appellant was deaf and dumb, mentally retarded, and totally incapable of communicating with people, including his lawyers. He had been charged with murder and was brought before the Magistrate's Court for what is known as a preliminary hearing to determine whether there was sufficient evidence to justify committing him for trial.

The Justices Act of the Northern Territory had certain provisions as to how such hearings were to proceed. For example, the law required the justice in charge of the hearing to ask the person being charged whether he or she wished to say anything in answer to the charge. It also required the justice to ask the accused whether he or she wished to call any evidence.

Now, the justice in this case realised that the accused (Ebataringa) didn't know what was going on and couldn't understand her, let alone respond to her questions. So she did the smart thing and referred the matter to a judge of

---

[21] Tuckiar v. The King (1934). 52 CLR 335.

the Northern Territory Supreme Court for a direction as to whether it was safe for her to proceed with the preliminary hearing. Despite the fact the Ebataringa couldn't talk, understand, or communicate with anyone, the judge said it was fine for the magistrate to proceed. People representing Ebataringa got together and appealed to the full Court of Appeal in the Northern Territory. Believe it or not, the three judges said it was OK for the magistrate to proceed with the hearing. Finally, Ebataringa's lawyers succeeded in getting leave to appeal to the High Court, which upheld the appeal and politely but unmistakeably chastised the judges of the Northern Territory Supreme Court.

In this context, let us see how the Northern Territory Supreme Court dealt with the Yolngu people's case.

6

The Conquering of David

I can't imagine that it is possible for anyone other than the indigenous people of this country to begin to understand the pain and hurt suffered by the Aboriginal people who, for nearly two hundred years, had to accept their characterisation of being "barbarous," "uncivilised," "lower in the order of things," "not capable of appreciating the benefits of British law," and goodness knows what other more disgraceful epithets. That is not to mention the physical manifestation of these perceptions involving dispossessing them of their land, forcing them to adapt to our laws, imprisoning them, and hanging them for disobedience while being blind to their spirituality and ancient cultures. And then holding them to account for not assimilating. That is not to mention the slaughter that characterised many of the fault lines between the arrival of the new owners of the land and its ancient occupiers.

After an amendment to our Constitution in 1967, which belatedly recognised the Aboriginal people as part of this country, our legal system had the opportunity for the first time in the post-1788 history of this country to make amends. But it passed up that opportunity. Faced with the overwhelming evidence that the assumption by the judges of the various courts of this country, including our High Court and the Law Lords of the Privy Council in England, that the indigenous people were barbaric and uncivilised was profoundly flawed, our legal system nevertheless clung to these myths.

With the coincidence of the Aboriginal narrative and the archaeological and anthropological discoveries in the middle of the last century, the Aboriginal movement gained sufficient confidence to confront our legal system with their stories of horrific oppression. The myth of terra nullius had been exposed. In its place evolved glimpses of an ancient civilisation that had cared for this land for tens of thousands of years and was bound to the land by a spiritual narrative of creation.

In 1968, the Yolngu people of Arnhem land petitioned the Supreme Court of the Northern Territory to stop the mining on their land by Nabalco, the multinational aluminium conglomerate. The Yolngu people claimed that they had an intimate affinity with the land, the origins of which reached back tens of thousands of years, when their ancestors cared for the land, paid tribute to its ancestral spirits, and kept alive the narrative of Aboriginal spirituality. Much more was at stake than a recognition of native title. Fundamental to the claim was a recognition of the history of the original inhabitants of this country.[22]

Nabalco had obtained licenses from the Northern Territory government to mine bauxite on land traditionally occupied by the Yolngu people. The Yolngu people decided that the time was ripe to defend what was left of their ancient and

---

[22] The case is officially known as Milirrpum v. Nabalco and the Commonwealth, 1971 FLR 146. However, I prefer to refer to it as the Yolngu people's case and will do so throughout this book.

sacred land. The progressive dispossession of the indigenous people of the land they occupied in 1788 had to stop. They assembled compelling evidence that demonstrated that the argument the country was unoccupied when the white man arrived was nonsense.

Nabalco was able to enlist the support of the Commonwealth government with the result that the Yolngu people found themselves confronted by the formidable armoury of a multinational company and the Australian government. Sadly, the traditions of our legal system and the malleable doctrine of precedent prevented the case from being a David slaying Goliath. But the institution of legalised dispossession didn't emerge unscathed.

Armed with the evidence of archaeologists such as W. E. H. Stanner (who we met in the previous chapter) and the narratives by the clan's elders of their continuous connection with the land over tens of thousands of years, the Yolngu people believed they had an unanswerable argument. They could prove that according to international law and English law as it stood in 1788, the indigenous people occupied this land. They were not a mob of uncivilised people without laws. They were a people with ancient and proud traditions. According to the Yolngu people, pre-1788 history should prevail over flawed post-1788 law.

Right at the start, there was something troubling me about the way the Yolngu people put their case. The Yolngu people came to the Australian court as supplicants on the basis that their ancestors became British subjects in 1788, and they were now seeking the protection of British law. This was at odds with another view of the relationship between the indigenous people and the white settlers. We will revisit this strategy when we talk about later cases.

Mr Justice Blackburn presided over the case, which involved forty-one days of sittings in which a range of evidence was submitted to the court from archaeological and anthropological insights into pre-1788 history to the narratives of some of the Yolngu people in their native tongues of the ancient stories that had been passed down through the centuries. There was a bit of a hiccup about the elders giving evidence of the stories of their ancestors. Nabalco claimed that the evidence was what we call "hearsay," which is not normally admitted in our courts. To his credit, Judge Blackburn allowed that evidence, which had to be translated into English.

Being the first case of its kind in Australian legal history, it is understandable that people were feeling their way, including the judge. The problem was the confounded doctrine of precedent. Being the first case of its kind in an Australian court, there were no previous decisions by Australian courts relating to native title. Nor were there any decisions of the Privy Council in relation to native title in this country. Furthermore, all the relevant decisions of the Privy Council were based on the assumption that the colonies were not occupied because of the low level of development of the native populations. By the time the Yolngu people's case came to court, there were no decisions of any courts with binding authority on the Supreme Court of the Northern Territory that addressed the new reality that this land was in fact occupied by the indigenous people in 1788 and not terra nullius.

If ever the stage was set for our courts to respond to new social phenomena, this surely was such a case. Judge Blackburn had a free reign, but he didn't seize the opportunity. Instead, he laboriously surveyed decisions of courts relating to the plight of American Indians, New Zealand Maori, and African natives all made on assumptions within the confines of legal theology developed in the high day of British colonialism, when natives were considered inferior people.

To his credit, Judge Blackburn gave the Yolngu people a fair hearing and indicated that he was impressed with the evidence of the elders and its reliability. But in doing so, he almost laid a trap for himself. So impressed was he with the evidence of the elders that he made a monumentally important finding. This is what he said:

> I am very clearly of the opinion upon the evidence, that the social rules and customs of the plaintiffs cannot possibly be dismissed as lying on the other side of an unbridgeable gulf. The evidence shows a subtle and elaborate system highly adapted to the country in which the people led their lives, which provided a stable order of society and was remarkably free from the vagaries of personal whim or influence. If ever a system could be called "a government of laws, and not of men" it is that shown in the evidence before me.[23]

---

[23] Millirrpum v. Nabalco 1971 (17) Federal Reports 141 at page 267.

In so finding, he rejected the Privy Council's view that natives were so low in the scale of social organisation, and so on, and he accepted that Australia at the time of the arrival of the First Fleet was not terra nullius.

Mr Woodward, QC, who argued the case for the Yolngu people, engaged Judge Blackburn at this point. His argument went something like this: If you reject the findings of the Privy Council that the natives were of such a low level of social organisation, and accept that this country was in fact occupied by the original inhabitants in 1788, how can you condone the taking possession of their land by the British?

That argument puts a cat among the pigeons because it challenges the legality of the dispossession. Realising the trap, Judge Blackburn pulled a number of rabbits out of the hat. He found that the Yolngu people had not occupied the land in question continuously and exclusively since 1788, but that was by the way.

In his research, Judge Blackburn came across comments by a George Chalmers. Mr Chalmers was a Scotsman who had studied law and emigrated to the American colony. He was a Royalist and supported the British in the War of Independence but then retreated to the United Kingdom. To say that he was a celebrated lawyer is gilding the lily, but he did write some stuff, including an incomplete book titled "Political annals of the present United Colonies; from their settlement to the peace of 1763."[24] It was to this undistinguished lawyer that Blackburn turned in order to

---

[24] George Chalmers, printed for the author and sold by J. Bowen, 1780.

rebut Mr Woodward's argument. Mr Chalmers argued that on bestowing sovereignty upon the overseas domains of the British Empire,

> It instantly became a fundamental principle of colonial jurisprudence, that in order to form a valid title to any portion of the general dominion, it was necessary to show a grant either mediately or directly from English monarchs.[25]

In other words, as the American Indians had not received a grant of land from the Crown of England, they could not establish title to their own land. Judge Blackburn embraced this as a jurisprudential underpinning of his argument that as the land of this country belonged to the Crown, and it had not made a grant of the land to the Yolngu people, they couldn't complain.

I would have to say that Mr Chalmers is not a household name in our legal history, and to use him as an authority for anything is to extend to him an unearned and undeserved credibility. But at the end of the day, it was of no avail as the judge found in favour of the mining giant and its friend, the Australian government.

This approach by Judge Blackburn led to the absurd proposition that the indigenous people occupied the land until 1788, but after that date, they could only obtain rights to their land if the king in England, in his wisdom, made a grant of that land to the indigenous people. The fact that

---

[25] *Political Annals*, vol. 1, p. 677, quoted at page 203 of the judgement of Judge Blackburn in the Yolngu people's case.

in the entire post-1788 history the king had made no such grant to the indigenous people meant that they had no right to their own land.

The official problem was what we call the doctrine of precedent, which we have touched on in pervious pages of this book. But it was so important to the result of this case that it is worth reminding ourselves of how it works. Lower courts are bound by the decisions of higher courts. For example, the Supreme Court of the Northern Territory is bound by decisions of our High Court, which is not bound by the decisions of any other court in the world. The High Court used to be bound by decisions of the Privy Council in England and of the House of Lords, but fortunately, that is no longer the case. Nevertheless, the High Court is still slow to disagree with decisions of the Law Lords in England.

Now, in the Yolngu people's case, Judge Blackburn inherited a lot of the dirty legal washing consisting of those decisions of the Privy Council, which we have already mentioned, and that were based on the unoccupied, uncivilised, barbaric terra nullius concept. But there were other precedents closer to home that were also predicated on the doctrine of terra nullius These were decisions of the Supreme Court of New South Wales and of our High Court.

One of the difficulties that the Yolngu people had to face was the fact that the doctrine of terra nullius was a product of the upper echelons of the English social hierarchy in which the monarch was supreme, if only notionally. Despite the constant diminution of the role of the sovereign in influencing policy since the Magna Carta and its consequential impotence, by attaching the imprimatur of the Crown to any act of His or Her Majesty's government, that act assumed the status of an edict from the High Priest in the temple. After the Americans attained their independence, there continued to be a contest between the Indians, who were the original inhabitants, and the government over land rights. These contests found their way into American law, but the circumstances of the Indians vis-à-vis their new landlords were quite different from those of the Australian Aborigines and the Australian government. Nevertheless, Blackburn embarked on lengthy references to American law as if it had anything to do with the case before him.

This is why we have to be very careful about a precedent in the law without knowing its origins. It was a principle of colonial jurisprudence that the monarch became owner of the new lands, and only the monarch could grant a title to that land. That raises the question of why it is a principle of colonial jurisprudence. The indigenous people had to wait until 1992 to get the definitive answer to that question. But according to Judge Blackburn, that was the state of affairs here once Captain Arthur Phillip arrived in 1788. However, Blackburn had to convert Chalmers's principle of colonial jurisprudence to contemporary Australia and relied on the decisions of the Privy Council and the High Court, already mentioned, and which were based on an assumption that Australia was terra nullius with the arrival of the First Fleet.

A comment by an undistinguished lawyer in relation to the colony of America in 1763 becomes the official doctrine of the highest court in the British Empire and now finds its way to the court of Judge Blackburn. Blackburn was clearly uncomfortable with the uncivilised and barbaric underpinning the Privy Council used to justify the doctrine of terra nullius. On one occasion he found it necessary to express his concern at what he believed to be an ignorance of the judges in England about the true nature of Aboriginal society before 1788. He referred to the following extract from a decision of Lord Sumner in the Southern Rhodesia case, which we have already noted.

> The estimation of the rights of aboriginal tribes is always inherently difficult. Some tribes are so low in the scale of social organization that their usages and conceptions of rights and duties are not to be reconciled with the institutions or the legal ideas of civilized society. Such a gulf cannot be bridged. It would be idle to impute to such people some shadow of the rights known to our law and then to transmute it into the substance of transferable rights of property as we know them.[26]

But he immediately followed that with his own observation that far from being uncivilised, the natives of this country had a highly developed system of laws. For the first time in our legal history, the fundamental perception of the nature of the indigenous people that formed the basis of dispossession was contradicted by a judge of an Australian court. The burden of precedent weighed heavily on Judge Blackburn in his 150-page judgement, which has been subject to much academic criticism.[27]

---

[26] In re Southern Rhodesia, 1919 AC p. 211 at pages 233–234.

[27] See, for instance, John Hooke, "The Gove Lands Right Case; A Judicial Dispensation for Taking of Aboriginal Lands in Australia, *Federal Law Review*, vol. 5, p. 85 et seq.

Despite what he might have thought personally of the English decisions and of our High Court on the subject of land ownership following 1788, Blackburn nevertheless considered himself bound by those decisions. This is Blackburn's reference to Australian authority:

> There is authority binding on this Court that at the moment when the Crown acquired sovereignty over land in Australia, that land became the property of the Crown in demesne, and so remained so long as it was not alienated. The High Court rested its decision on this basic principle in Williams v. Attorney-General for New South Wales (1913) 16 C.L.R. 404 (), where the question was whether the public had a right, as against the Crown, to have the Government House domain in Sydney used as a residence for the Governor of New South Wales. Barton A.C.J. said (at p. 428): "Waste lands of the Crown, where not otherwise defined, are simply, I think, such of the lands of which the Crown became the absolute owner on taking possession of this country as the Crown had not made the subject of any proprietary right on the part of any citizen." Isaacs J. said (at p. 439): "It has always been a fixed principle of English law that the Crown is the proprietor of all land for which no subject can show a title. When colonies were acquired this feudal principle extended to the lands oversea. The mere fact that men discovered and settled

> upon the new territory gave them no title to
> the soil. It belonged to the Crown until the
> Crown chose to grant it.[28]

In summary, when Captain Phillip arrived here in 1788, King George III became owner of the lands of this country until he gave it away by means of a Crown grant. This aspect of the case was seriously debated by counsel for the Yolngu people. Judge Blackburn had put himself into a corner. In the Privy Council case of Cooper v. Stuart,[29] according to Blackburn, "the Board founded itself upon the proposition that the colony of New South Wales belonged to the class of settled colonies."

You will recall that in the previous chapter, there was a reference to this decision of the Privy Council in which the Law Lords decided that at the time of the arrival of Captain Phillip, New South Wales was a tract of largely unoccupied land when it was peacefully annexed to the British dominion.

Now, this statement didn't sit kindly with Blackburn's finding that this land was in fact occupied by a sophisticated people. Mr Woodward QC persisted in his attempt to engage the judge on this point. He continued to ask the question, "How can an authority based on a false appreciation of the facts have any binding influence given what we know today about the indigenous people?" Judge Blackburn answered it by continuing to rely on the decision of the Privy Council and escaped from the trap with the following reasoning:

---

[28] Yolngu people's case, p. 245.

[29] Cooper v. Stuart, 1888, AC 286 at page. *(Due to the author Louis Coutts' illness, full details can't be provided)*

> The question is one not of fact but of law. Whether or not the Australian aboriginals living in any part of New South Wales had in 1788 a system of law which was beyond the powers of the settlers at that time to perceive or comprehend, it is beyond the power of this Court to decide otherwise than that New South Wales came into the category of a settled or occupied colony.[30]

I must admit to bemusement at this dismissal of Woodword's argument. Legal principles have to relate to facts. Every case brought before our courts involves a set of facts, and it is up to the court to relate legal principle to these facts. Blackburn was confronted with the contradiction between the evidence that Australia was not terra nullius, or if you like, "unoccupied" in 1788 and the rulings of the Privy Council and our own courts that it was, resulting in the land becoming the possession of the Crown. Nineteenth-century legal principle was founded upon a grotesquely erroneous perception of the true state of occupation of this country in 1788.

Put another way, the legal principle that the land of this country became the possession of the English Crown to the exclusion of the then-inhabitants was founded on a false premise. Quite simply, the premise was that in 1788 the land was unoccupied, whereas the opposite was in fact the case. The reality deprives the decisions on which Judge Blackburn relied of any legal credibility. It would have been easy for Blackburn to distinguish those cases as having

---

[30] Yolngu people's case supra, p. 243.

no relationship to the facts of the case over which he was presiding, but he balked at that opportunity and dutifully followed a flawed precedent.

In fairness to Blackburn, he was faced with a momentous dilemma. If he surrendered to the reality that this country was not terra nullius in 1788, it might open a Pandora's box. The safest option was to blindly follow discredited precedent and decide there was no principle in English law that recognised native title. Indeed, complete ownership of the land by the Crown in 1788 made it impossible for anyone else to have an interest in the land.

In the end, Blackburn's thesis for rejecting the claim of the Yolngu people was that at the time Captain Cook proclaimed sovereignty over this country, the land became the possession of the Crown. Subsequent decisions confirmed in Blackburn's mind that at that stage, the land in this country was owned by the Crown. He dismissed the Yolngu people's claim by saying, "It was the contention of counsel for the defendants that the principle enunciated in all these cases is exhaustive; the Crown being the absolute owner in demesne of all unalienated lands, there is no room for any doctrine of communal native title. As the plaintiffs cannot show a title derived from a Crown grant, they must fail."[31]

Perhaps this summary of the case by Judge Blackburn could be described as the "Cook and Phillips" theory of sovereignty. It is impossible to avoid the conclusion that the basis on which he found that there was no such thing as

---

[31] Ibid.

native title recognised by our law was that Cook and Phillip had successfully transferred all the land in this country to King George III. It is an embarrassing and preposterous basis for establishing a principle of law and declaring it a precedent.

The first attack on the citadel ended in tragedy. Let us see if there is any accuracy in the statement of Karl Marx that "History repeats itself first as tragedy, second as farce."

7

An Unequal Contest

It took some time for the indigenous people to digest the bitter pill of rejection in the Yolngu people's case. On the one hand, they would have been buoyed by Judge Blackburn's finding that at the time of the arrivals of Captain Cook and Captain Phillip, the country was in fact occupied by a people governed by a system of laws. On the other hand, they would have been devastated at Blackburn's slavish following of a Privy Council decision based on an assumption that the indigenous people were uncivilised without any system of law. In 1977, the contradiction found its way into a claim by an Aboriginal lawyer, Paul Coe, who sued both the British and Australian governments. In the document that formed part of his claim, this is what he said:

> On or about a day in April 1770 Captain James Cook RN. at Kurnell wrongfully proclaimed sovereignty and dominion over the east cost of the continent now known as Australia for and on behalf of King George III for and on behalf of what is now the second named Defendant (The Australian government).

> 3A. On or about the 26th day of January, 1788 Captain Arthur Phillip, RN. wrongfully claimed possession and

occupation for the said King George III on behalf of what is now the second named Defendant of that area of land extending from Cape York to the southern coast of Tasmania and embracing all the land inland from the Pacific Ocean to the west as far as the 135th longitude including that area of land now occupied by the first named Defendant at the Commonwealth Offices, Sydney, Commonwealth Bank Building, Martin Place, Sydney.

3B. The claims of Captain Cook, Captain Phillip and others on behalf of King George III and his heirs and successors were contrary to the rights, privileges, interests, claims and entitlements of the aboriginal people both individually and in tribes and of the aboriginal community and nation as more fully set out in 8A hereof.

Mr Coe was mindful of the fact that in the Yolngu people's case, they submitted themselves to English and Australian law on the basis that they became British subjects in 1788. As that didn't work, Mr Coe took another approach and argued that the indigenous people never surrendered sovereignty to the Crown back in 1788 and that King George III and his subjects had no right to take over the country.

Before giving more attention to Mr Coe's claim, I decided I should find out exactly what Captain Cook said and what Captain Phillip was commissioned to do on his arrival in New South Wales.

On the April 29, 1770, Captain Cook planted the English flag at what was named Botany Bay, and on August 22, he did the same on Possession Island in Torres Strait. On the day he planted the English flag on Possession Island, he entered the following statement in his journal:

> Notwithstand[ing] I had in the Name of his Majesty taken posession of several places upon this coast I now once more hoisted English Coulers and in the Name of His Majesty King George the Third took posession of the whole Eastern Coast from … Latitude [38° South] down to this place by the Name of New South Wales together with all the Bays, Harbours Rivers and Islands situate upon the said coast after which we fired three Volleys of small Arms which were Answerd by the like number from the Ship. (The spelling is that of Captain Cook which may or may not have been correct at the time).

Following is part of the commission to Captain Phillip, which he read at Sydney Cove on the January 28, 1788:

> With these Our Instructions you will receive Our Commission under Our Great seal constituting and appointing you to be Our Captain General and Governor in Chief of Our Territory called New South Wales extending from the Northern Cape or Extremity of the Coast called Cape York in the Latitude of Ten Degrees thirty seven

Minutes south, to the Southern Extremity of the said Territory of New South Wales, or South Cape, in the Latitude of Forty three Degrees Thirty nine Minutes south, and of all the Country Inland to the Westward as far as the One hundred and Thirty fifth Degree of East Longitude, reckoning from the Meridian of Greenwich including all the Islands adjacent in the Pacific—Ocean within the Latitudes aforesaid of 10° 37' South, and 43° 39' South, and of all Towns, Garrisons, Castles, Forts, and all other Fortifications, or other Military Works which may be hereafter erected upon the said Territory, or any of the said Islands, with directions to obey such Orders and Instructions as shall from time to time be given to you under Our Signet and Sign Manual, or by Our Order in our Privy Council; You are therefore to fit Yourself with all convenient speed, and to hold yourself in readiness to repair to Your said Command, and being arrived, to take, upon the execution of the place and trust We have reposed in You, and as soon as conveniently may be with all due solemnity to cause our said Commission under our Great Seal of Great Britain constituting you Our Governor and Commander in chief as aforesaid, to be read and published.

These words didn't come under the legal microscope until Mr Coe's case in 1977. As a result, for two hundred years, they were the fundamental bedrock on which the current institution of Australia was founded. I am not quite sure what these words mean. There was an assumption from the time of the arrival of Captain Cook that the territory of New South Wales was "ours," meaning the Crown's. These words had the magical quality of dispossessing the current inhabitants of their land and making them subject to English law. Not one indigenous person at the time had the faintest idea of what was happening.

As occupation expanded, the effect of these words in reinforcing the proposition that English law became the law of this land, and that the land became the domain of the king, were endorsed both by local courts and the Privy Council, which was the final court of appeal from Australia. As we discovered in the discussion of the Yolngu people's case, there was an assumption on the part of the newcomers that sovereignty as well as ownership of the land passed to the king in 1788. There was a total absence of any awareness, a total ignorance of Aboriginal civilisation by the newcomers that has persisted to this day, albeit by a diminishing community.

Sadly, this ignorance, rather than any Act of State on the part of the British colonisers, became the justification for the dispossession of indigenous lands and the corruption of their civilisation.

For people like me, nurtured in the traditions of Western civilisation, it is impossible to comprehend the anger and pain the Aboriginal community must suffer as a result of the grotesque treatment inflicted on them over the past two hundred years. In reading Mr Coe's statement of claim in his action against the British and Australian governments, that anger and sense of injustice emerges in emotional rather than technical legal language. But in this uncelebrated case, the chasm of misunderstanding between the established community and the Aboriginal people was finally institutionalised in our legal system. As a result, Mr Coe, the plaintiff, and Mr Justice Gibbs, the defendant of our British institutions, were at cross purposes, talking different languages. Mr Coe talked the language of pain, and Judge Gibbs talked the language of an emotionally affronted representative of our constitutional institutions who could only cling to precedent.

Mr Coe's argument was, "How can these acts and words of Captain Cook and the words in Captain Phillip's document have the profound consequence of disinheriting the current inhabitants of their land, wiping out their culture and making them subject to British law without them having the faintest idea of what was going on?" According to Mr Coe, the land was occupied by an ancient civilisation with its own laws, religion, spirituality, and economy. According to him these words of Captain Cook and Captain Philip had no effect; they were just words. As we have seen, he had some support from both international law and English common law.

Mr Coe ran into some problems. From reading his documentation, I suspect that his emotional sense of injustice became a substitute for the technical legal language of our traditional English common-law system. He was berated by Judge Gibbs for the use of such language in our court system. However, the Australian government used a ploy to prevent his argument ever seeing the light of day in a court.

The government asked the High Court to dismiss Mr Coe's case without a hearing. The case came before four judges of the High Court, but Gibbs gave the definitive judgement. He understood what the case was all about when he said,

> If the amended statement of claim intends to suggest either that the legal foundation of the Commonwealth is insecure, or that the powers of the Parliament are more limited than is provided in the Constitution, or that there is an aboriginal nation which has sovereignty over Australia, it cannot be supported.[32]

He followed this up with one sentence in which he dismissed the claim:

> The annexation of the east coast of Australia by Captain Cook in 1770, and the subsequent acts by which the whole of the Australian continent became part of the dominions of the Crown, were acts of state whose validity cannot be challenged: see New South Wales v. The Commonwealth [1975] HCA 58; (1975), 135 CLR 337, at p 388, and cases there cited.[33]

I visited the New South Wales case and was disappointed to discover that the two cases on which Gibbs relied in making that statement were decisions of the Privy Council in England that have forever tarnished the jurisprudence

---

[32] Coe v. The Commonwealth (1979) HCA 68.

[33] Ibid.

of our common law. I will deal with them in chapter 9, but suffice to say that in 1970, the House of Lords distanced itself from those decisions.

According to Judge Gibbs, Mr Coe's claim was the type that could not be contested in our courts. The very nature of the claim deprived it of the right of a hearing. And so that was the end of that argument. Not only that, because it was a decision of the High Court that binds every other court in the country, the decision cannot be challenged. As a result, the validity of the annexation of this country by George III cannot ever be challenged. That principle of law, which is called the doctrine of Act of State, became a lifeline for the High Court in the later and more famous case of Mabo v. The State of Queensland. However, the legal mystery remains. How can a British sailor claim possession of this land on behalf of a monarch in England by simply planting the British flag in its soil? In Mr Coe's case, the High Court refused to answer the question. It went further and decided that the original inhabitants had no legal right to challenge the actions of Captain Cook, Captain Phillip, and the British government in taking possession of the land and proclaiming British law as the law of the land.

It is always disturbing for a lawyer when the law prevents a client from seeking redress at law. If a wrong has been done to a client, there is an expectation that the law will provide a remedy. The expedition and brevity with which Gibbs dismissed Mr Coe's case and the significance of the decision to the indigenous people prompted me to undertake a journey of exploration in some depth to discover the reasoning behind his decision. The doctrine of Act of State in the hands of Judge Gibbs assumed an extraordinarily powerful status in our law. It is so powerful that it denies people the right to seek redress for wrongs inflicted on them. Even though our courts dismiss jurisprudence as irrelevant in their decision-making process, such a principle that our courts will not address a wrong is not only a novelty in the history of our jurisprudence, it affronts the basic concepts of justice.

On my journey I discovered that the Act of State doctrine had its origin in the affairs of the notorious East India Company. Not only was the doctrine fake, it had absolutely no relevance to the cases of Mr Coe and Mr Mabo, yet the High Court relied on it to deny the indigenous people the right to challenge the legitimacy of sovereignty.

The journey took me back to the seventeenth century. It also resulted in making discoveries about the notorious activities of the East India Company on which Gibbs relied in dismissing Mr Coe's claim. Before we take this journey into a notorious passage of English common law, it is desirable to visit a more famous indigenous case, the case of Mabo v. The State of Queensland (No 2).[34]

---

[34] Mabo v. The State of Queensland, No. 2 (1992) HCA 23.

8

Playing by the Rules

Just imagine that you and your friends have been saving up for years, and then a group representing themselves as investors come along and heavy you into investing your savings with them. After a while, you realise that they haven't invested the money on your behalf but have distributed it to a lot of their mates. You kick up a fuss, and they respond by saying that they feel very sorry for you and are prepared to help you. However, there is one condition they insist on before providing help. The condition is that they make the rules, and if you are going to seek help from them, you have to accept their rules.

"So, tell us what your rules are?"

"Well, the first rule is that you can't challenge the validity of what we have done."

You reply, "But you guys have robbed me, and you are saying that you are going to help me only if I don't complain about the fact that you have robbed me."

"That's it in a nutshell. It is up to you. If you want us to help you, you just have to accept that what we have done is OK. You are not going to get your money back, but there might be a consolation prize."

You reply, "But that is cheating. You take our money and give it to your mates, and you won't let us challenge that. We just have to accept that you have taken our money, and you aren't going to give it back."

"Take it or leave it. It is all the same to us."

You have nowhere to turn, so you have to go along with these crooks in order to get their so-called help. It is a bit like going into the ring with your two arms tied behind your back and knowing the referee is on the side of your opponent.

Welcome to Mabo versus the State of Queensland, or the descendants of the original inhabitants of this country versus the newcomers.

We have seen how the Yolngu people tried to have the law recognise their traditional occupation of their land, but the Northern Territory Supreme Court knocked them back because English rules were against them. Then Mr Coe had a go, arguing that the declaration of sovereignty over this country and the dispossession of the natives was illegal. We have learnt that argument didn't even get him to first base.

Now, in 1982, a gentleman by the name of Eddie Mabo, from the island of Mer in Torres Strait, confronted with this 2–0 defeat, took comfort from some of Judge Blackburn's observations that the indigenous people were civilised, and as a result, the land was not unoccupied in 1788. Mr Mabo made another attempt to turn back the tide. He claimed that he and his people had been traditional owners of the land on the island for many generations and had continued to occupy the land in very specific ways since 1788. They asked the court to recognise their possession of the land by way of native title. The brief history is interesting.

> On 20 May 1982, Eddie Koiki Mabo, Sam Passi, David Passi, Celuia Mapo Salee and James Rice began their legal claim for ownership of their lands on the island of Mer in the Torres Strait between Australia and Papua New Guinea. The High Court required the Supreme Court of Queensland to determine the facts on which the case was based but while the case was with the Queensland Court, the State Parliament passed the Torres Strait Islands Coastal Islands Act which stated "Any rights that Torres Strait Islanders had to land after the claim of sovereignty in 1879 is hereby extinguished without compensation."[35]

Judge Brennan, who delivered a judgement supported by two of his fellow judges, summarised the essential elements of the case: "Oversimplified, the chief question in this case is whether these transactions had the effect on 1 August 1879 of vesting in the Crown absolute ownership of, legal possession of and exclusive power to confer title to, all land in the Murray Islands."[36]

The case finally came before the High Court.[37]

---

[35] See https://aiatsis.gov.au/ntpd-resource/28875.

[36] Mabo v. The State of Queensland (No 2), HCA 23 paragraph 23 of the Judgement of Brennan CJ.

[37] Mabo v. The State of Queensland (No 2), ibid.

Mr Mabo's claim was quite adventurous because back in 1971, as we have learnt, Mr Justice Blackburn in the case of the Yolngu people decided that English law did not recognise native title, so Mr Mabo was kicking against the wind as the saying goes. There was this problem. The newcomers had taken the land from the indigenous people and weren't about to give it back. If Mr Mabo was able to establish that there was such a thing as native title, and it was recognised by English law, it could open myriad difficulties. What would happen to all the land that had been given to the newcomers? After all, there was the Sydney Opera House built on land that used to be occupied by the indigenous people before Captain Cook came along. Not to mention the millions of buildings around the country on land owned by people who had their title to the land registered in title offices in the different states.

By bringing his case in an Australian court, as was the case with the Yolngu people, Mr Mabo had agreed to play by the rules of the very people who had robbed the indigenous people of their land. By the time Mr Mabo's case reached the High Court, it was common knowledge in Australian society that the argument of terra nullius was dead, and this country had been inhabited for tens of thousands of years by an ancient civilisation before the arrival of Captain Cook. From a social and political point of view, the court would have looked ridiculous if it had prolonged the myth of terra nullius.

Mr Mabo had a few problems, as did the High Court. Mr Mabo was not going to get anywhere if the High Court decided it was bound by decisions of the Privy Council of the nineteenth century based on the doctrine of terra nullius.

The High Court would look foolish if they followed these decisions, which meant that the High Court would have to break with precedent. But then the court would be in a catch-22 situation. If it followed precedent, it would be enshrining the unsustainable argument that the land was terra nullius at the time of the arrival of Captain Cook. That would make the court look stupid. If it didn't follow precedent and accepted that the land was not terra Nullius, then it would open the door for the indigenous people to say that the dispossession was illegal, and that simply couldn't happen.

If the High Court were to allow a claim for native title, it had to do so without opening the floodgates of claims that the dispossession was illegal. The court had to have a bet each way. It had to accept that Australia was not terra nullius when Captain Cook planted his flag and Captain Phillip read his commission. Such a finding would destroy the underpinning of the decisions of previous centuries that assumed the natives were barbarous and uncivilised. The legal infrastructure that lent its imprimatur to the dispossession was faulty. If Mr Mabo were able to convince the High Court to ignore, if not overrule, those decisions, the very validity of the dispossession would be in question. That is where Mr Coe's case and the East India Company cases came in handy. But before we return to that, let us look at how Judge Brennan dealt with the problem.

The first issue he had to deal with was the doctrine of terra nullius. He invoked the assistance of a judge of the International Court of Justice in an advisory opinion in relation to Western Sahara.[38] In that case, Judge Ammoun traced the origin of the doctrine to an Italian authority on international law, Pasquale Fiore, who was born in 1837. He regarded terra nullius territories as those inhabited by populations whose civilization, in the sense of the public law of Europe, is backward and whose political organization is not conceived according to Western norms. In this Western Sahara case, Judge Ammoun was at pains to put this doctrine to bed and was assisted by one of the counsel in the case who rejected this materialistic definition. In quoting counsel, this is what Judge Ammoun had to say about terra nullius:

> Mr. Bayona-Ba-Meya goes on to dismiss the materialistic concept of terra nullius, which led to this dismemberment of Africa following the Berlin Conference of 1885. Mr. Bayona-Ba-Meya substitutes for this a spiritual notion: the ancestral tie between the land, or "mother nature", and the man who was born therefrom, remains attached thereto, and must one day return thither to be united with his ancestors. This link is the basis of the ownership of the soil, or better, of sovereignty. This amounts to a denial of the very concept of terra nullius in the sense of a land which is capable of being appropriated by someone who is not born therefrom. It is a condemnation of the modern concept, as defined by Pasquale Fiore.[39]

---

[38] Western Sahara (1975) ICJ R.

[39] Ibid., p. 85.

How on earth, in the face of this condemnation of the doctrine, could our High Court in 1992 persist with the myth that had disinherited the indigenous people of this country? Their spiritual link to the land conferred upon them "sovereignty." An extension of this argument meant that on the arrival of Captain Cook, the indigenous people possessed sovereignty over this country.

Judge Brennan was clearly troubled by the legal consequences of accepting the idea of the indigenous people being sovereigns of the land. He had some wonderful things to say about the issue that perhaps were intended to comfort the indigenous people. You might recall the reference earlier to a decision of the Supreme Court of New South Wales in 1848, in which the judge decided that the law of England became the law of the land in 1770, and the king became owner of the land. Brennan dismissed that view of the law with the following evocative language:

> If the conclusion reached by Stephens CJ
> (Brown) be right, the interest of indigenous
> inhabitants in colonial hands were
> extinguished as soon as British subjects
> settled in a colony, though the indigenous
> inhabitants had neither ceded their land
> to the Crown nor suffered them to be
> taken as the spoils of conquest. According
> to the cases, the common law itself took
> from indigenous inhabitants any right to
> occupy their traditional land, exposed them
> to deprivation of the religious, cultural
> and economic sustenance which the land
> provides, vested the land effectively in the

control of Imperial Authorities without any right to compensation and made the indigenous inhabitants, intruders in their own homes and mendicants for a place to live.[40]

Brennan continued with encouraging, if condescending, comments to the indigenous people. The following comment may have been interpreted by them as an expression of indignation on the part of the High Court at their treatment:

> The facts as we know them today do not fit the "absence of law" or "barbarian" theory underpinning the colonial reception of the common law of England. That being so, there is no warrant for applying in these times rules of English common law which were the product of that theory. It would be a curious doctrine to propound today that, when the benefit of the common law was first extended to Her Majesty's indigenous subjects in the Antipodes, its first fruits were to strip them of their right to occupy their ancestral lands.[41]

That was precisely the argument Mr Coe wanted to put to the court but was prevented from doing so. However, Brennan had a lot more to say in order to put the genie back in the bottle. There is a temptation to interpret these

---

[40] Mabo v. The State of Queensland (no 2) (1992) 175 CLR 1 at page. *(Due to the author Louis Coutts' illness, full details can't be provided)*

[41] Ibid., p. *(Due to the author Louis Coutts' illness, full details can't be provided))*

comments as accepting that the indigenous people were sovereigns of this country in 1788 and that they occupied the land in a manner that brought the land within the protection of international law as land "occupied."

In making those concessions, Judge Brennan decided it was necessary to salvage the situation. He had to face two momentous issues in Australian law. This land was occupied by the indigenous people in 1788, and according to international law, even though the indigenous people were unaware of the fact, they were sovereigns of the land. The first issue was clearly the question of how this sovereignty passed to the Crown in 1788 without the knowledge of the indigenous sovereign people. If Brennan could overcome that problem, he then had to confront the nineteenth-century principle that with sovereignty passing to the Crown, so did the ownership of the land. If the king became owner of the land in 1788, that would put an end to any claim to the land by the natives.

Judge Brennan decided that the key to unscrambling this conundrum was to address the issue of sovereignty. If the Crown's sovereignty over this land was questionable, then the whole edifice of our constitutional arrangements would be in question and this was the danger point in the case, as it was in Mr Coe's case. It had to be put to bed.

But how on earth do you get over the admission that in 1788, the indigenous people were sovereigns of the land? The answer was simple. According to Judge Brennan, "The Crown's acquisition of sovereignty over a particular part of

Australia cannot be challenged in an Australian municipal Court."[42]

Brennan quoted Judge Gibbs's observations, which we recorded in discussing Mr Coe's case, as the authority for this statement. In two sentences, one by Gibbs and one by Brennan, indigenous sovereignty was surrendered to the Crown, and the indigenous people were denied the right to any challenge. As a result, in the history of Australian law, the constitutional question of the validity of sovereignty by the Crown has never been argued in an Australian court, nor can it be. We can be grateful for the achievements of the East India Company in it gaining the approval of the Privy Council for its Acts of State, which consisted of divesting Indians of their wealth.

But there was one case[43] that Brennan relied on as an authority that drew my attention. It is such an absurd reference that I will refer to it separately in the following chapter. It suffices at this stage to indicate that one of the judges in the case on which Brennan relied specifically cautioned against treating the case as establishing a principle of law.

It is difficult to understand how this statement can be used as authority for arguing that the proclamation of sovereignty over Australia by Captain Cook cannot be challenged in an Australian court. In any event, it may seem pedantic, but in Mr. Coe's case, Judged Gibbs decided that the, "annexation of the East Coast of Australia," was an Act of State that cannot be challenged. He did not specifically mention the

---

[42] Ibid., p. *(Due to the author Louis Coutts' illness, full details can't be provided)*

[43] *The Fagerness*, 1927, p. 311, 43 TLT.

issue of sovereignty. It is also sad that just as Gibbs had ignored many of the leading and recent cases on Act of State, so did Judge Brennan. But that is now history. By putting the issue of sovereignty beyond reach of Mr Mabo and the indigenous people of this country, the way was clear for the court to let the indigenous people have the crumbs from the rich man's table. Those crumbs were to become known as native title. To do so, he had to overcome the nineteenth-century principle that the king became owner of the land in 1788.

Before we move to this issue of native title, it is fair to say that the legality of the sovereignty of the Crown over the people who occupied this country in 1788 and their land has never been contested in any court on this planet, nor can it be according to Judge Brennan. By refusing the indigenous people permission to challenge the legality of sovereignty, the High Court has put to bed forever and beyond legal challenge the spurious claim to sovereignty by the Crown as a result of the planting of flag in Botany Bay and on Possession Island in 1770 and the reading of his commission of the Crown by an army captain on the January 26, 1788.

To deal with the land question Brennan came up with a master stroke of legal engineering to overcome this problem.

It is interesting that neither Judge Gibbs nor Judge Brennan addressed the legality of the Crown's claim to sovereignty. They simply ruled that it could not be challenged. The preservation of that fiction formed the fortress for defending the legality of what the newcomers to this country had done since 1788. Once they had to accept the new rules that they could not challenge sovereignty, the indigenous people had to be happy to accept the crumbs offered them by Brennan. So, thank goodness for the East India Company.

As the Crown became sovereign of this land no later than 1788, all its inhabitants became subject to British law. Ridiculous though that sounds, Brennan had covered himself by saying that no one could challenge that ridiculous proposition. The indigenous people then understood what playing by the rules meant. They were the rules of the robber.

Having put the issue of sovereignty to rest, all Brennan had to do was address the issue of annexation.

The next step in the process of giving some crumbs to the indigenous people was to say the early decisions that suggested the king became owner of the land in 1778 were incorrect. All that happened in 1788, when sovereignty over this land passed to the Crown, was that the king acquired what has become known as a "radical" title to the land. That takes some understanding, and I would have to say that I can't personally get my head around it. However, according to Brennan, it goes something like this:

On the proclamation of sovereignty over the land, the validity of which can't be challenged, the Crown did not become owner of the land but simply had political control over the land to do with it what the king liked. If he granted the land to the newcomers, which he did, that was his right as sovereign. Once he granted the land, the person to whom the land was granted became complete owner of the land to the exclusion of anyone else. But before the king made a grant of land to the newcomers, as he only had a radical title to the land, it came with the baggage of pre-existing native title. The radical title possessed by the Crown was said to be "burdened" by native title. But because the king had sovereignty over the country and its people, he could do what he liked with the land, despite the fact that he didn't own it. Accordingly, once he gave the land to the newcomers, native title was extinguished.

I continue to have another difficulty with this explanation of radical title. By making a grant of land encumbered by native title, the king conferred on the grantee of the land greater rights than those possessed by the king. While the king held a radical title, the land was encumbered by native title, but by giving the land away, that right of native title disappeared, and the grantee ended up with complete ownership. Property lawyers can probably explain how someone can give to another person rights that they do not possess themselves.

If that is not complicated enough, it becomes more complicated, and I have to admit to not understanding the next stage. It is a chicken-and-an-egg situation. According to Judge Brennan, native title only survived if indigenous people could prove that they had occupied the land without interruption since 1788, together with the continuity of their culture and traditions. If they couldn't prove that, native title, to use the words of Brennan, had been "washed away by the tide of history." But because the king had radical title, he could give the land on which the aboriginal people had traditionally existed with their spirituality and culture to the newcomers by way of a crown grant. Once a grant was made, the newcomers would kick the aboriginal people off the land, which meant they could no longer qualify for native title according to the new rules of Brennan. In other words, by granting the land to the newcomers, the Crown was destroying native title. The king could do this because it was impossible to challenge the legality of sovereignty. And it is all thanks to the East India Company and its incestuous relationship in the eighteenth and nineteenth centuries with the Privy Council and is its influence in Parliament.

However, for the Murray Islanders there was a happy ending. When Europeans discovered the Murray Islands, they were not interested in the land. They found pearls and ravaged the sea surrounding the islands of its precious treasures. Almost by accident, the Murray Islanders were left to occupy the land without invasion. They thereby passed through the eye of the needle of Brennan's formula for qualifying for native title. And everyone celebrated this as a great victory for the indigenous people. But what this case did was to legitimise the dispossession of the indigenous people of this country and completely closed the door on their right to challenge the theft.

Brennan's judgement was decorated with quite a few intellectual observations enhanced by extracts from the dead language of Latin. Following is one such quotation:

> The characteristic of feudalism "is not tenere terram, but tenere terram de X" (81) Pollock and Maitland, The History of English Law, 2nd ed. (1898, reprinted 1952), vol.1, p 234n. It is implicit in the relationship of tenure that both lord and tenant have an interest in the land: "The King had 'dominium directum', the subject 'dominium utile'" (82) ibid., p 773; Co Litt

> 16. Absent a "dominium directum" in the
> Crown, there would be no foundation for
> a tenure arising on the making of a grant
> of land.[44]

I know that the Aborigines are the best linguists in the country, but if they can understand a word of this nonsense, they are certainly world class.

There is another aspect of this case that disturbs me. Brennan referred to 231 reported decisions of courts around the world going back as far as 1683. Let us assume that it took Brennan an hour to read each case (in my experience, some cases necessitate constant revisits to fully understand them), it would have taken at a very minimum 230 hours to read those cases without necessarily analysing them. If Brennan devoted five hours a day without interruption to read those cases, it would have taken him forty-six days just to read them. It is improbable in the extreme that he did so, and more likely than not, he had no more than a fleeting acquaintance with some of those references. This raises the question of the reliability of the references.

That is not the main vice of this indulgence in esoterica. He was talking to the Aboriginal people who had developed their own laws of this country over tens of thousands of years. Despite that, they had to sit down and listen to a judge of our High Court tell them what their rights were based on over two hundred decisions of courts in the system of English law. Because of this fragile but tenacious defence

---

[44] Mabo ibid., p. *(Due to the author Louis Coutts' illness, full details can't be provided))*

of the doctrine of sovereignty, there was not an opportunity for the descendants of the original inhabitants to say, "We are not interested in your law. We are not interested in what happened somewhere else in 1683. We want you to listen to our law."

In all of the decisions in relation to native title, lip service has been paid to Aboriginal law. The entire legal enterprise has involved pleading in Australian courts that English and Australian law provides a fragile legal fig leaf that forever prevents the indigenous people from challenging the central legal issue that separates them from their heritage, and that is the legality of sovereignty. According to the High Court, sovereignty has enabled the crown to extinguish native title and it therefore legitimises forever the dispossession.

The indigenous people are expected to celebrate the decision of the High Court in Mabo v. The State of Queensland.

Judge Brennan's judgement was supported by two other judges. Another two judges, Deane and Gaudron, delivered a separate but joint judgement. Dawson delivered a separate judgement, disagreeing with the other six judges. Toohey delivered a separate judgement. Accordingly, their Honours adhered to a well-established practice of failing to present a unified approach to one of the major issues to confront the High Court. While such disagreement is disturbing, it stimulates reflections, which unveil profound concerns as to the integrity of the technical underpinnings that support the various findings. In the next chapter, I indulge in my own reflections on this tragic episode in the history of the original inhabitants of this country.

In summary, in Mabo, the High Court decided:

1. That the Crown become sovereign of this country on the proclamation of Captain Cook in 1770.
2. That the descendants of the original inhabitants are prohibited from challenging the legality of the Crown becoming sovereign.
3. At the time the Crown became sovereign, the land was subject to native title, and ownership of the land did not pass to the Crown despite two hundred years of law and practice that treated the land as owned by the Crown.
4. With the passing of sovereignty, the Crown obtained what is described as a "radical title" to the land, which was said not to amount to ownership but a political right to do with the land as the Crown pleased. The radical title was said to be burdened by native title.
5. Because of sovereignty, the Crown could do what it liked with the land, and to the extent that it made grants to newcomers and conferred on them a clear unencumbered title, they became owners of the land against all people.
6. To the extent that the Crown exercised its sovereignty in making grants of land to the newcomers and more recently selling the land, native title to that land was extinguished. In the words of Brennan, native title has been, "washed away by the tide of history."

This amazing framework of legal architecture is supported by one pillar, and that is the proposition that sovereignty passed to the Crown in 1770. As I indicated in the introduction, the proposition that a unilateral act of a sailor conferring sovereignty on the Crown of England over a country occupied for tens of thousands of years by an indigenous civilisation without their consent affronts my concepts of Anglo-Saxon jurisprudence. This so-called Act of State, which the indigenous people are prohibited from challenging in our Courts, is the legal fig leaf that validates the history of this country since 1788.

If the indigenous people were permitted to challenge the legality of sovereignty in our courts, what would be the outcome?

9

Act of State: The Myth

Two profoundly fundamental issues were avoided by the High Court in the cases of Mr Coe and Mr Mabo. Until they are resolved, the legal relationship between the descendants of the original inhabitants and the formal government institutions of this country will remain the source of continued irritation.

The first issue involves an examination of the so-called doctrine of Act of State and the extent of its applicability in our courts. The second involves an examination of the constitutional validity of the proclamation of sovereignty over this country as a result of the acts of Captain Cook and subsequent events. The refusal to address the first issue has enabled the court to avoid having to address the second. So what was it that Judge Gibbs said in dismissing Mr Coe's claim without a trial?

> The annexation of the east coast of Australia by Captain Cook in 1770, and the subsequent acts by which the whole of the Australian continent became part of the dominions of the Crown, were acts of state whose validity cannot be challenged.[45]

---

[45] Coe v. The Commonwealth, 1979, HCA 68.

Normally, such a sweeping statement of the law with such profound consequences is preceded by a tedious judicial examination of all the precedents relied on to support the statement. But nothing of the sort preceded this statement in Mr Coe's case: "You can't bring your case in this court." Pressed for some explanation of his statement, Gibbs went on to say:

> The annexation of the east coast of Australia by Captain Cook in 1770, and the subsequent acts by which the whole of the Australian continent became part of the dominions of the Crown, were acts of state whose validity cannot be challenged: see New South Wales v. The Commonwealth [1975] HCA 58; (1975), 135 CLR 337, at p 388, and cases there cited.[46]

I visited the New South Wales case, and there tucked away in a lengthy dissenting judgement of Gibbs was this statement:

> The acquisition of territory by a sovereign state for the first time is an Act of State which cannot be challenged, controlled or interfered with by the courts of that state. For statements and illustrations of this principle it is enough to refer to Salaman v. Secretary of State in Council of India (1906) 1 KB 613, esp at pp 639–640; Sobhuza II v. Miller (1926) AC 518, and Secretary

---

[46] Ibid.

of State for India v. Sardar Rustam Khan (1941)_AC 356, esp at pp 370–371.[47]

In Mr Mabo's case, Brennan referred to this statement of Gibbs for his authority for making the following statement: "The Crown's acquisition of sovereignty over a particular part of Australia cannot be challenged in an Australian municipal Court."[48]

To the casual observer, it may appear that these two judges are saying the same thing, but in fact, there is a subtle and profound difference in these statements. Gibbs believed he was making a correct statement of the law that had been in place for the two hundred years since the arrival of the First Fleet. He used the phrase, "acquisition of territory," indicating that the Crown had acquired the land of this continent in 1770. Brennan distanced himself from that statement and used the phrase, "The Crown's acquisition of sovereignty." What he was doing was turning his back on two hundred years of the Crown making grants of land based on the legal theory that as of 1770, the Crown owned the land.

Brennan added two more cases that he claimed to be authorities for this statement. In two sentences, supported by a couple of footnotes, the dreams of the indigenous people of restoring legitimacy to their tenure to this land were dashed. Rather than take their Honours' words for granted, I took myself off to the law library to check out the authorities

---

[47] New South Wales v. The Commonwealth, 1975 HCA.

[48] Ibid at p. *(Due to the author Louis Coutts' illness, full details can't be provided)*

relied on by Their Honours for these sweeping statements. I was not prepared for my discoveries.

The cases referred to by Gibbs were just the tip of the iceberg. My research unearthed case after case of the most spectacular stories of plunder, greed, corruption, and theft associated with a not inconsiderable amount of killing. The origins of the statements of Gibbs and Brennan are to be found in the decisions of the Privy Council in England legitimising every notorious activity of the East India Company. The Gibbs' doctrine of Act of State had its origins in a dark period of English jurisprudence; I have traced the origins back to a decision of the Privy Council in 1791. Before I tell you the story of that case, let me tell you something about the East India Company. From now on, let's call it "the Company."

During the reign of Queen Elizabeth in the year 1600, the Company was granted the monopoly over the trade in spices in the Indies. Gradually, by Royal Charter, its powers were dramatically extended, and it was granted the right to represent itself in India as the government of Great Britain. The British government had privatised itself so that the Company became its representative in India and ultimately the British Raj. Part of its authority involved, "the sole privilege of trading in India and the right to send men and ships etc., and to commission officers to continue to make war and peace for their advantage, with any natives not Christian."

Effectively, that gave to the Company the right to do what it liked in India—so long as it was dealing with non-Christians—and that is precisely what it did. To support its "trading" activities, the Company had its own army that could conquer and take possession of the wealth of India in the name of the Crown but on the basis that the Company and its employees retained most of the ill-gotten gains.

Over the years, as its army grew and a gentleman by the name of Robert Clive headed up its army in India, the Company conducted the most powerful protection racket in history. It had a simple formula. It would knock on the door of the local nawab and say something like, "I have a deal for you." The deal was that the nawab hand over his assets in exchange for protection and a stipend. These deals were done as representatives of the British government and called treaties. They were called treaties because, according to the Privy Council, the nawab was considered to be head of a sovereign state, despite the fact that he lacked most of the trimmings of a sovereign. And when it suited the Company, he became subject to British law. A recent commentator with extensive knowledge of the Company summed up its operations thus:

> We still talk about the British conquering India, but that phrase disguises a more sinister reality. It was not the British government that seized India at the end of the 18th century, but a dangerously unregulated private company headquartered in one small office, five windows wide, in London, and managed in India by an unstable sociopath—Clive.[49]

---

[49] See https://www.theguardian.com/world/2015/mar/04/east-india-company-original-corporate-raiders by William Dalrymple.

The Company was a trading company, and it operated to extend the territory of the Crown in India, while at the same time, taking possession in its own right to India's wealth. The technique of its protection racket was the use of its extensive army, supported by English munitions, to extract concessions from the wealth of the nawabs of the country. This was also the company that developed such a relationship with the Privy Council that it could continue its operations in India with legal impunity. To the outside observer and many members of Parliament at the time, including Edmund Burke, the case that came before the Privy Council in 1791 should have been the opportunity to put an end to the Company's rapacity. But they didn't bargain for the ingenuity of the Law Lords who heard the case of The Nabob of Carnatic v. The East India Company.[50]

It is customary for reports of court decisions in the English legal world to set out the facts that give rise to the case and for judges to identify the facts they consider relevant to their decisions. The Nabob of Carnatic case was the first in the line of cases relied on by the High Court in rejecting the right of the indigenous people to challenge the legitimacy of the proclamation of sovereignty over this county on behalf of George III. For some reason that has never been explained, the Law Lords in this case departed from the practice of reciting the facts. There was no mention of the facts giving rise to the decision. I have gone to some trouble to establish those facts. In an article[51] by Pavarthi Menon is a summary of perhaps the most iniquitous financial scandal in history. She provides some details of the "loans" made by employees

---

[50] The Nabob of Carnatic v. The East India Company 1 Ves June 371.
[51] *Review of Agrarian Studies*, vol. 9, no. 1, January–June 2019.

of the Company to the nabob to enable him to pay his so-called debts to the Company.

The nabob of Carnatic, who commanded vast wealthy possessions, was having difficulty with his neighbour, the Raja Ali. The Company, which had its eyes on the possessions of the nabob and the raja, came along and did a deal with the nabob. They would clean up the raja and continue to provide protection to the nabob. When the dust had settled, they sent the nabob a bill requiring him to pay a huge amount which the Company said was the cost of the war with the raja. In addition, the Company required the nabob to pay annual fees for continued protection. The amount of money involved was huge. The fees soon exhausted the nabob's cash reserves, and he was unable to meet the Company's demands for cash.

Employees of the Company came to the nabob and told him that they could help him. They would lend him the money so that he could pay the Company. What followed was so disgraceful that it beggars imagination. These employees of the Company who became lenders required security for the loans, which attracted interest rates of up to 24 per cent. The nabob assigned properties to these lenders, which consisted of farmland leased to farmers. The lenders then extracted increased rents from the farmers, who defaulted, and the employees then became owners of the land.

As the nabob's situation became more desperate, loans were negotiated, but the employees refrained from paying the principal of the loan for two years, during which time the interest received equalled the amount of the loan and was handed over to the nabob as the principal. The Company stepped in and quantified the loan at £294,000 at a new interest rate of 12 per cent in respect of which not a single rupee had been advanced to the nabob. At one stage, the nabob's total debt in relation to which very little had been advanced in the way of capital, was estimated to be £4.4 million in those days, which is an astronomical sum by today's standards. In addition, the employees had made a killing in taking possession of the farms as a result of the default of the farmers.

This is how Edmund Burke described the scandal in a speech in Parliament:

> By what means could a number of slight individuals, of no consequence ... without the command of armies or the known administration of revenues ... in a few years (as to some even in a few months), amassed revenues equal to the revenues of a respectable Kingdom?

In 1801, the Company took possession of the nabob's remaining assets.

These were the circumstances leading to the legal action taken by the nabob against the Company, which resulted in the decision of the Privy Council in 1791. I have gone to some trouble to give a brief summary of the facts of this case to place in context the decision of the High Court to rely on a series of similar decisions by the Privy Council to justify refusing the indigenous people of this country a right to contest the legality of sovereignty and dispossession.

The nabob finally had enough and issued proceedings against the Company. He claimed that rather than him owing money to the Company, the Company owed him money, which undoubtedly was the case. Accordingly, he asked the court to order that the Company make disclosure of the documents of their "loan" transactions and that a person be appointed to audit the relevant accounts. It was a pretty straightforward case. The nabob wasn't claiming any money, although he did intend to seek recovery of money if the examination of the documents and the statement of accounts indicated the Company was indebted to him.

The Company was represented by the attorney general, who went on and on with archaic language and reference to procedural rules that we don't understand today. But basically, he was saying that as the relationship between the Company and the nabob was between two separate sovereign people, and therefore an Act of State, the court could not hear the case. One of his arguments was that it was the practice of the directors of the Company in England to provide secret instructions to its officers in India. If in carrying out those instructions they could be challenged in a court, then their secrecy could be exposed.

The judge, after hearing hours upon hours of argument, had enough and decided that as the dispute between the parties arose out of a treaty between two sovereign people and was an Act of State, the court could not hear the case. The treaty was an Act of State, which could not be challenged in an English court. The judge would have none of the arguments of the lawyers for the nabob. They argued that the process of the Company and its employees usuriously and unscrupulously robbing the nabob had nothing to do with a treaty but was just daylight robbery. They argued that the real nature of the relationship would be revealed if the court allowed inspection of documents.

In a moment of exasperation, when the lawyers for the nabob were not getting anywhere with the Lord Chancellor, the leading lawyer exclaimed, "I do not dispute their power to rob any of the powers in India; but that is an odd reason to prevent the Court from decreeing them to pay their debts."[52] In other words, nothing can be done about the Company robbing my client, but surely they have to pay their debts.

Those arguments fell on deaf ears. The Lord Chancellor who decided against the nabob could not have been unaware of the outrage by people throughout England—including members of Parliament, such as Edmund Burke—at the operations of the Company. Perhaps that is the reason he refrained from setting out the facts of the case. The decision legitimised the ongoing corruption in which the Company progressively raped India of its wealth, and in the light of events can legitimately be described as corrupt. The doctrine of Act of State was simply a device to immunise the activities of the Company from the scrutiny of the courts.

I wonder what the court would have decided if the boot was on the other foot? Suppose the nabob refused to pay the so-called debt to the Company. Would the Privy Council have let the nabob off the hook?

---

[52] Ibid.

This was the first in a series of cases, including the case quoted by Gibbs, where the Company welched on its deal to pay the nawab a pension.

But there were others.

As the activities of the Company became more sophisticated on the political, legal, and extortionist levels, by 1843, even the local courts in India came on board and relied on the Act of State rabbit to excuse even the most aberrant behaviour of the Company. In 1843, a case came before the Supreme Court of Bombay. Some locals sued the Company for trespass and breaking and entering. Ordinarily, it would be a crime that, if committed in England, would result in a no-return ticket to the convict settlement in Australia. However, the judge of the Supreme Court of Bombay found that as the breaking and entering was authorised by the governor of Bombay, it was an Act of State, so the court had no jurisdiction to hear the case. Actually, the governor of Bombay and the Company were both representatives of the Crown and were, therefore, one and the same thing.

When you think that things couldn't get worse, they did. In 1859, a case[53] came before the Privy Council on appeal from the Supreme Court of Madras. The raja of Tanjore died without leaving a male issue or a will. However, he was survived by his widow. The raja had acquired massive wealth, and when he died, the widow claimed that according to Hindu law, she was entitled to his estate. (She and her children would also have been entitled to his estate according

---

[53] Secretary of State in Council for India v. Kamachee Boye Sahaba, 1859 7 Moo, I. A, 476.

to the English laws of intestacy.) The Supreme Court of Madras agreed with her, so the Company appealed to its old friend the Privy Council, claiming that as the directors of the Company had passed a resolution on the death of the raja claiming an entitlement to his entire estate, they had performed an Act of State, which the widow could not challenge in any court in the British Empire. It is interesting that the attorney general for England, rather than appearing for the Crown, appeared for the widow and slammed what he said was the outrageous attempt to fill the coffers of the Company with ill-gotten gains. But Lord Kingsdown, of the "barbarous" fame, would have none of it.

There had been the usual protection treaty with the raj, but there was nothing in the treaty that provided for the destiny of his assets upon his death. The seizure of his estate was a unilateral act on the part of the directors of the Company. There is no doubt that the Company eyed the wealth of the raja and set its mind on acquiring that wealth. There were polite comments about looking after the widow, but in the end, the Privy Council authorised the transfer of the assets of the raja of Tanjore to the East India Company.

But it was worse than that. Our friend Lord Kingsdown set out to record some of the most infamous passages in the literature of the English common law. This is how he justified the transfer of the wealth of India to the Company:

> In the year of 1855, the East India Company, in the exercise of their sovereign power, thought fit, from motives of State, to seize the Raj of Tanjore and the whole of the property the subject of the suit, and did

seize it accordingly and that over an act so done, whether rightfully or wrongfully, no municipal court has any jurisdiction.

He referred to the case of the nabob of Carnatic as his authority for this statement.

So there you go. Once the East India Company has decided to seize assets from motives of state, the unlucky owner of those assets can't challenge the seizure in a British court. There was no pretence at legalities such as treaties between sovereign people. It was a decision that prevented the widow from challenging an avaricious and illegal grab of property.

Even Lord Kingsdown realised the insult to jurisprudence by indicating that the act of seizure was quarantined from legal challenge, whether rightfully or wrongfully. But he went on to add insult to injury. Towards the end of his judgement, when he realised the absurdity of finding for the Company, this is what he said:

> Of the propriety or justice of that act, neither the Court below nor the Judicial Committee have the means of forming or the right of expressing, if they had formed any opinion. It may have been just or unjust, beneficial or injurious, taken as a whole to those whose interests are affected. These are considerations into which their Lordships cannot enter. It is sufficient to say, that even if a wrong has been done, it is a wrong for which no municipal court of justice can afford a remedy.

In summary, "We don't care how good your case is or how much wrong has been done, we are simply not going to let you have your case heard in one of our courts." In short, this decision was a license for the Company and the Crown to do what they liked with impunity, and that is precisely what they did. But there is something profoundly wrong with this decision.

Occasionally in the development of our law there are moments in legal history when new and unexpected phenomena arise for which there is little or no precedent. On those rare occasions, courageous judges have fallen back on a fundamental principle of our jurisprudence to ensure that where there is a wrong, there should be a remedy.

Lord Kingsdown trampled on a principle of English jurisprudence that reached back to 1215, when King John, confronted by hostile barons who were sick of their wealth being purloined to fund the king's enterprises in France and the Holy Land, signed a document forever known as the Magna Carta. Clause 40 stated, "no free man shall be taken or disseised or outlawed or in anyway ruined … except by the lawful judgement of his peers or by the law of the land." That was supposed to be an end to what might be called unilateral authoritarianism. Every Plantagenet king was required to swear allegiance to Magna Carta at his coronation.[54]

It is a cornerstone of English common law that no person shall be deprived of their property or liberty other than in

____

[54] See Dan Jones, *The Plantagenets* (Harper Press, 2012), pp. 209–218.

accordance with the law. To maintain that the law does not provide a remedy when a person is robbed by the Crown is an affront to the Magna Carta and the integrity of our legal system. However, after the decision of Lord Kingsdown, the Company and the Crown had carte blanche. There was no longer any need for fig-leaf protection of a treaty or to justify the Act of State trick. So long as the Company or the Crown acted with motives of the state, the act of seizing property could not be challenged in an English court. The cases I have described formed the basis on which Gibbs specifically relied in dismissing Mr Coe's case.

The first case[55] relied on by Gibbs is one of the more shameful decisions in English law.

Back in the days of the Company in the 1830s, it decided that the Punjab was a great source of wealth. But the locals kicked up a fuss, and there was a war. The locals nearly pulled it off, but in the end, the Company's army reassembled and won the day. That resulted in some so-called treaties between the nawab and the Company that required the nawab pay the costs of the war and to continue to pay for the protection the Company would provide. The nawab died in 1839, and his three oldest sons died under mysterious circumstances, leaving his five-year-old son as his sole heir. The Company then entered into a "treaty" with the guardians of the five-year-old, which effectively assured him of protection on the basis that he hand over his assets, and in return, the Company would pay him a pension for life. On his death many years later, the beneficiary of the boy's will discovered that the Company had welched

---

[55] Salaman v. Secretary of State in Council of India (1906) 1 KB 613.

on paying the pension and owed an amount of about £300,000 to his estate. The trustee of the boy's estate sued the secretary of state for India, which was the successor in title to the Company. The Privy Council had no difficulty in dismissing the claim on the basis that the agreement to pay arose out of a treaty between two sovereign peoples, which was an Act of State, and as a result, English courts had no jurisdiction to hear the case.

The next case[56] on which Gibbs relied reflects some of the darker moments of the British Empire in Africa.

The king of Swaziland had granted a lease of fifty years to some ministers of the church on the condition that a portion of the land was to be reserved for use by local natives. The ministers sold the lease to some people who intended to use the land for commercial farming. However, they found that part of the land was occupied by the natives for whom it had been preserved by the king. Some sleight of hand then took place. Swaziland was a separate country. It had not been conquered; it had not ceded sovereignty to or entered into a treaty with the Crown. However, because the English had just cleaned up the Boers in the Boer War in South Africa, South Africa became firmly part of the British Empire. As South Africa had traditionally used its muscle to get Swaziland to do its bidding, Swaziland became what was called a protectorate. So when these farmers took possession of the land and found the natives in the way, some funny things happened. Firstly, the Crown, by order in council, declared certain lands, including those leased to the farmers and subject to the rights of the natives, to be Crown land.

---

[56] Sobhuza II v. Miller (1926) AC 518.

Once having got hold of the land, the Crown, through the local governor, transferred the land previously held by the farmers back to them. The farmers then kicked the natives off the land. The local natives kicked up a fuss and rather stupidly appealed to the Privy Council. In a few paragraphs, the Privy Council decided that the acquisition of the land by the Crown was an Act of State, and accordingly, the locals were prevented from making a claim in the courts.

There was no beating about the bush. No invocation of treaties between sovereign states. The simple act of stealing the land was an Act of State and beyond challenge.

But Gibbs was not finished. To his eternal shame, he quoted another case[57] that supported his rejection of the right of the indigenous people to challenge sovereignty. In 1903, the khan of Kalat handed over in perpetuity to the British governor general in his region a great deal of land that was said to be under his control. However, before doing so, he had transferred certain land to a certain person who had in turn transferred the land to Sardar Khan, who successfully sued the governor in the local court in India, which held that the agreement between the khan and the governor could not have the effect of transferring to the Crown land that had already been transferred to someone else.

The Privy Council took no time in finding for the Crown. The agreement was an Act of State and could not be challenged in an English court. The Privy Council did not deal specifically with the difficult question that the Sadar Khan was not a party to the agreement on which the Crown

---

[57] Secretary of State for India v. Sardar Rustam Khan (1941) AC 356.

relied; nor was the person from whom he obtained the land. The Act of State doctrine prevented him from asserting his right to land that was legally his.

The forgoing is a summary of the wealth of authority on which Judge Gibbs relied in refusing Mr Coe permission to challenge the proclamation of sovereignty over this country. It was accepted by Blackburn in the Yolngu people's case that this country was not conquered in 1788, there was no treaty between the then inhabitants and the Crown, and the then-inhabitants did not cede their country to the Crown. According to Blackburn, the country was occupied by a sophisticated people with their own laws, spirituality, and economy. English law forbade the acquisition of occupied territory other than by treaty or by cession. According to English law, the law of a conquered country was to continue until altered by Parliament.

It is impossible to glean from any of the cases quoted by Gibbs, or the cases referred to in those cases, any support for Gibbs's rejection of Mr Coe's claim. Mr Coe was claiming in an Australian (formerly a British) court that the proclamation of sovereignty over this country was prohibited by English law. All that was asked was that an English court should apply English common law, which stated that the annexation of occupied territory was prohibited.

10

Mabo and the Act of State

As we discovered in dealing with the case of Mr Mabo, Judge Brennan quarantined any challenge by the indigenous people to the legality of the proclamation of sovereignty and relied on the authorities quoted by Judge Gibbs, which we have just visited. However, he added two more authorities, and it is extremely disappointing to discover that neither authority has any relevance to the East India Company Act of State doctrine. It is an embarrassing illustration of how sometimes judges make observations based on so-called authorities who turn out to be unreliable.

The first of the additional cases[58] relied on by Judge Brennan for his breathtaking statement was a case involving a collision between Italian and English ships in the Bristol Channel. The collision occurred at a point where the channel was over thirty kilometres wide. The question arose as to whether the collision occurred in English territorial waters or in international waters. When the case came before the Court of Appeal in England, their Lordships requested advice from the attorney general who, after research and consulting the Home Secretary advised the court that it was the view of the Home Secretary that the collision did not occur in territorial waters.

---

[58] The Fagerness, 1927, p. 311, 43 TLT.

Three judges heard the case, and in three separate but brief judgements decided to accept the evidence of the attorney general. One judge decided that the opinion of the Home Secretary did not bind the court but was evidence to which great weight should be attributed. In the end, he accepted the evidence and found that the collision did not occur in English territorial waters.

A second judge, in an equally brief decision, did find that he was bound by the evidence of the attorney general but hastened to add that his decision should not be interpreted as deciding a point of law.

The third judge took the view that he should not ignore the evidence of the attorney general and accordingly, decided that the collision occurred in international waters.

The term "Act of State" was not mentioned throughout the case and certainly not by any of the judges. The case had nothing to do with denying parties jurisdiction or the right to bring their case in an English court. It had absolutely no relevance to the so-called doctrine of Act of State that prevents parties from bringing proceedings in an English court.

If that wasn't bad enough, Judge Brennan referred to an Australian case[59] that involved determining whether a citizen of New South Wales should be extradited to New Guinea to face a charge of murder. The case, which was quite simple but provided Judge Latham in particular with the opportunity for complication, involved whether the

---

[59] Ffrost v. Stevenson (1937), HCA 538.

Fugitive Offenders Act or the Service and Execution Act applied. It also involved examining two provisions of the Constitution, one relating to service and execution and the other to the foreign affairs power of the Commonwealth. In the end, Mr Frost was extradited to New Guinea.

The relationship that this case has to a doctrine that prevents parties from access to the courts is beyond me.

11

What the High Court Missed

It was one thing for the High Court to dismiss Mr Coe's case out of hand without providing a legal rationale for the rejection. All that Gibbs really said in Mr Coe's case was, "You cannot challenge sovereignty in this court." Brennan effectively repeated the rejection. Both referred to cases that at the very most had doubtful relevance and, in reality, did not support the proposition of Gibbs. There was no explanation as to how these cases supported the rejection of Mr Coe's claim. That was all bad enough, but to totally ignore a principle of Act of State that had stood the test of time both in English and American law for 350 years was unforgiveable.

In 1674, an interesting case came before the Court of Chancery in England. By the seventeenth century, monarchs around the world had perfected the concept of monopolies. It was a pretty simple process whereby the monarch would "sell" a monopoly to some entrepreneur. In this 1674 case,[60] the king of Denmark had granted a monopoly to a Mr Blad, a Dane, to fish in the waters off Iceland. Despite this, an enterprising Englishman by the name of Bamfield fished in those waters and had his catch taken by Mr Blad, who was defending his monopoly. Later on, Mr Blad travelled to England, and Mr Bamfield sued him for the value of the

---

[60] Blad v. Bamfield 36 ER (1674) 992.

fish that he had taken from him. Mr Bamfield claimed that Mr Blad had illegally taken possession of his fish.

The Court of Chancery in England decided that as Mr Blad had acted in accordance with the law of Denmark, the court had no jurisdiction to hear the case. The reason was quite simple. An English court cannot rule on the validity of an Act of State of a foreign power. You can imagine how ridiculous it would be if an Australian applied to an Australian court to decide that a law of New Zealand was invalid. The court would rightly say that it had no jurisdiction to hear such a case. This was still considered to be a fair statement of the law in relation to the doctrine of Act of State as late as 1964[61] in the United States and 1970[62] in England.

It is a shame that Mr Coe and Judge Gibbs overlooked a long line of decisions in relation to the traditional definition of the doctrine of Act of State as established in 1674. There were two cases in particular that might have helped.

One was a decision of the English Court of Appeal (effectively, the House of Lords) in 1970. It was a case in which the House of Lords finally turned its back on the sad, mutated doctrine of Act of State.[63] A Mr Nissan, an English gentleman, conducted a hotel on the island of Nicosia at the height of the conflict between Turkey and Greece. The British Army sent out its troops and commandeered Mr Nissan's hotel. After they left, the hotel was in a mess, and the government refused to pay for the accommodation or the repairs. Sound familiar?

---

[61] Banco Nacional de Cuba v. Sabbatino, 376 U.S. 398 (1964).

[62] Nissan v. The Attorney General [1970] AC 179.

[63] Ibid.

The government pleaded Act of State. This time it didn't work. The court refused to follow the precedents that we have just been discussing and on which Gibbs and Brennan relied. But it went further and decided that an Act of State is no defence to a claim by a British subject in relation to a wrong inflicted by the government. If the government does harm to a British subject, it can't claim the protection of Act of State. These days, it just has to pay up.

That case really put an end to the nonsense dished out by the Privy Council in the heyday of the Company. It was decided before Mr Coe's case, but Gibbs made no reference to the decision. Nor did he make any reference to a decision of the House of Lords in 1921.[64]

In another case, an Irishman, who was an American citizen, was arrested in England and charged with illegal drilling. When arrested, the police took from him about £130. On his release, he claimed the return of the money, and typically, the British government refused to pay, claiming that the taking of his money was an Act of State. That didn't wash with the House of Lords. According to the House of Lords, an alien resident in England is subject to English law. That being the case, an alien must also enjoy the benefits of English law. According to English law, an Act of State is no defence to a claim for damages by a British subject. Nor is it a defence to a claim by an alien resident in the country and subject to its law. At long last, the English court put a stop to the unjust enrichment that had fed the pockets of those associated with the East India Company.

---

[64] Johnstone v. Pedlar (1921) A C 262.

Another case to which no reference was made in Mr Coe's case was a decision of the US Supreme Court in 1964.[65] It involved an arm of the Cuban government suing an American bank. It was held that a foreign sovereign state could sue in an America court. This was a case in which an American citizen seized Cuban assets on the basis that they were rightfully his but had become the possession of the Cuban government when it nationalised the sugar industry. He claimed that the nationalisation of his sugar assets in Cuba was illegal. The US Supreme Court, following that ancient case of Blad v. Bamfield,[66] held that it could not rule on the validity of an Act of State of a foreign power, in this case, the Cuban government. It also held that it was lawful for a foreign power to bring proceedings in an American court to protect its interest.

Subsequent to the decisions in Coe's case and Mabo, a lawyer writing in the *Melbourne International Law Review*[67] traced the history of the doctrine of Act of State, and in a thorough review of cases, did not mention any of the cases relied on by Gibbs or Brennan in the later case of Mabo.

It must have been abundantly clear to Gibbs that the precedents on which he relied and subsequently were relied on in the case of Mabo to prevent the indigenous people from challenging sovereignty had been discredited by the highest court in England. The extent of their relevance to modern legal theory was demonstrated in

---

[65] Banco Nacional de Cuba v. Sabbatino, 376 U.S. 398 (1964).

[66] Blad v. Bamfield 36 ER (1674) 992.

[67] Mathew Alderson BA, LLB (Hons) (Macq); LLM (UCL), *Melbourne Journal of International Law*, vol. 12 (2011).

an article published in the *Colombia Law Review.*[68] The author, who is perhaps the leading British legal historian, quotes a definition of an Act of State by another legal historian[69] but immediately proceeds to quote the following qualification:

> This definition is supplemented by his further statement that there can be no such thing as an act of state as between the sovereign on the one hand, and his subjects or those who owe him temporary allegiance on the other.

For centuries, the indigenous population of this country was forced to show an allegiance to the Crown. Countless thousands have been incarcerated according to English and more recently Australian law, and goodness knows how many have gone to our gallows. The Crown, under the pretext of sovereignty, has taken their land, and they are told they have no legal remedy.

It must be a hard pill to swallow for the descendants of the original occupiers of this land to have to come cap in hand to a court that is a creature of the institutions that have taken their land. It must hurt even more when that court simply says, "You can't bring your case in our courts."

---

[68] William S. Holdsworth, The History of Acts of State in English Law, *Columbia Law Review,* vol. 41, no. 8 (Dec. 1941), pp. 1313–1331.

[69] Stephen, *History of the Criminal Law of England* (1883). *(Due to the author Louis Coutts' illness, full details can't be provided)*

I may have this all wrong, but to refuse the indigenous people the right to air these arguments in our courts without giving reasons or a legal analysis perpetuates the disdain with which the indigenous people have been treated since 1788.

12

Mr Coe: The Sequel

It is very late in the day, and the tide has certainly gone out so far as the rights of the indigenous people to their own land is concerned. The practicalities of their circumstances are largely irreversible, but to prevent the descendants of the original inhabitants from at least arguing their case in our courts by virtue of a couple of dismissive sentences of two judges of the High Court, based on the most dubious authorities, leaves a vacuum in the jurisprudence of this country that aches for attention.

This vacuum will not be filled by nomenclature, by changing a word in our National Anthem, or by invoking words such as "invasion." The problem is more profound, and its solution has to embrace a journey back in timelessness to those first moments of the origin of the beliefs of the indigenous people, when out of the Dreaming emerged a civilisation founded in stories and beliefs and centred on the spirituality of the land. In 1788, more than forty thousand years of history was represented by the people who inhabited this land on the arrival of the First Fleet. Within a few short years, that civilisation was devastated.

One of the world's great sculptures is the *Pietà* by Michelangelo. For centuries it has remained resplendent in St Paul's Basilica in Rome. Then, in 1972, an Australian believing he was Jesus Christ took to it with a hammer. By the time he was restrained, marble pieces of the sculpture were scatted on the floor of the Basilica. The world was devastated by the wanton act of destruction of such a sacred monument to the Renaissance heritage. Some people in the church at the time stole many of the pieces of marble.

In 2014, ISIL embarked on an orgy of destruction of ancient religious sites constructed over three thousand years ago, and the world was aghast. Remnants have either been stolen or become rubble.

These are two of many examples of the horror with which people of the Western tradition respond to wicked acts of violence against precious heritage.

Recently, mining giant Rio Tinto decided to destroy two 46,000-year-old Aboriginal rock shelters in order to access $135 million worth of iron ore that would not have been available under alternative mining plans that would have avoided the culturally significant site. It was on the news for a few days, and the executives of Rio apologised. There was a parliamentary inquiry, and of course, everything has now settled down, and Rio is still in the business of mining.

As a white person with only the most fleeting appreciation of Aboriginal culture, I find it difficult to understand the lack of bewilderment at the breathtakingly incomprehensible and unfathomable depth of the extinction of the Aboriginal heritage, which is now almost non-existent. Two hundred years of Western occupation of this country wiped out more than forty thousand years of civilisation. The ghastliness of the crime, no matter how unintentional, is beyond imagination. This is the evil event that cries for recognition and understanding. To dismiss the indigenous people's claim in two sentences brings little credit to our High Court. Admittedly, in the case of Mr Mabo, three judges included some apologetic language in their judgements but nevertheless clung desperately to the legality of British sovereignty to excuse themselves.

While the destruction of the Aboriginal heritage in this country is irreparable, its meaningful recognition is surely an essential step towards establishing recognition of the current indigenous people as survivors and beneficiaries of the original inhabitants. This can only be achieved by an honest and scrupulous judicial examination of the legality of the proclamation of sovereignty over this country between 1770 and 1778. Perhaps Mr Coe, better informed and better advised, could start his case anew today.

Perhaps he could enlist the aid of current elders to sign declarations that they can trace their origin back to their elders in 1788 and sign a declaration that they authorise Mr Coe (or whoever now assumes the mantle) to represent them in claiming that their clan never surrendered its sovereignty to the English Crown. Aided by the narratives of elders and the assistance of archaeologists and anthropologists, as was the case in the Yolngu people's case, he then files a statement of claim in one of our federal courts. His claim is that he acts on behalf of the descendants of the original inhabitants as of 1788, and because neither the original inhabitants nor their descendants have ever conceded their sovereignty to the Crown of England, their country has never been conquered, and they have never entered into a treaty with the representatives of the Crown, they are entitled to the protection of the laws of this country and accordingly seek a declaration that according to the law of England in 1788, the proclamation of sovereignty over this country on behalf of the Crown of England by Captain Cook and subsequent events had no legal effect, and the descendants of the original inhabitants are the rightful sovereign people of this country.

Supposing the judges of the federal court try and pull the Act of State trick out of the hat. But by this time, Mr Coe and his lawyers are awake, and the case ends up in the High Court. The High Court would have to confront some legal realities if it was going to invoke the Act of State doctrine to dismiss the Aboriginal challenge. They would be forced to recognise that there are in fact two Act of State doctrines, one which is authentic and has stood over three hundred years. The other is a fake doctrine that has had a rocky road over the last two hundred years and has not been followed by the highest court in England.

First, let us look at the genuine doctrine. Since 1674, it has been the law of England and followed by the Supreme Court of the United States that our domestic courts will not entertain a challenge to an Act of State of a foreign power. In England, the Court of Chancery refused to entertain a challenge to an Act of State of Denmark granting a monopoly on fishing in Danish waters to a Danish citizen. In America, the Supreme Court refused to entertain a challenge to the validity of an Act of State of the Cuban government privatising the sugar industry. They were Acts of State of foreign powers within their own jurisdictions and could not be challenged in our courts. This makes abundant sense.

This principle had no application to the argument of the Aboriginal people. They would be challenging an Act of State of our own government as successor in title to the British government in our own court system.

Despite the fact that before the fake Act of State doctrine it had already been rejected by the Court of Appeal in England, it became the underpinning of the basis for refusing the ability of the Aboriginal people to challenge sovereignty in our courts.

Since 1791, it has gone through various iterations by the Privy Council, and it is difficult to state the fake doctrine with any clarity. However, in 1791 the Privy Council refused the right of the nabob of Canatic to sue the East India Company on the basis that the dispute arose out of a treaty between two sovereign people.

For that Act of State trick to work, there has to be a dispute between two sovereign people who are party to a treaty. This would involve the government recognising the Aboriginal people as a sovereign people, which is precisely what they claim to be. Furthermore, the government would have to identify a treaty, which of course, it can't do.

That leaves the cupboard bare. There is no Act of State doctrine that prohibits the Aboriginal people from challenging sovereignty in our courts.

The government would be stuck with a further problem. In cases involving historical events, such as the case of the husband charged with raping his wife in 1963, the court is obliged to apply the law that was in existence at the time. In other words, what was the law in 1963?

In considering whether sovereignty passed to the Crown between 1770 and 1788, the court would be obliged to apply the law as it stood in 1788. Not any of the East India Company cases had been decided at that stage, and the only indication of the law as it stood then was English common law and international law, which we have already visited and which established that sovereignty does not pass in relation to occupied territory.

In this context, it is worthwhile to repeat what Sir William Blackstone wrote in 1765:

> So long as it was confined to the stocking and cultivation of desert uninhabited countries, it kept strictly within the limits of the law of nature. But how far the seizing on countries already peopled, and driving out or massacring the innocent and defenceless natives, merely because they differed from their invaders in language, in religion, in customs, in government, or in colour; how far such a conduct was consonant to nature, to reason, or to Christianity, deserved well to be considered by those, who have rendered their names immortal by thus civilizing mankind.[70]

---

[70] *Sir William Blackstone's Commentaries.*

We also know that this was a tenet of international law in 1788.[71]

Accordingly, the court would be confronted by evidence that this country was occupied by a sophisticated people in 1788, that it had not been conquered, that no treaty had been signed between the Crown and the then-inhabitants, and they had not ceded their country to the Crown. The High Court could not call on the subsequent decisions of the Privy Council refusing to permit the defrauded Aborigines to pursue their claims in court. In any event, as we have seen, subsequent legal developments have resulted in those decisions being relegated to the dust heap of the history of the common law.

To prevent the current Mr Coe from arguing his case, the High Court would have to pull a rabbit out of the hat themselves as the East India rabbit wasn't living in 1788.

The proclamation of sovereignty by Captain Cook was a unilateral act made without the consent or knowledge of the then-occupiers of the land. It was a pre-Magna Carta act of monarchical authoritarianism. The court would be confronted with the knowledge that the inhabitants had not ceded sovereignty to the Crown and that their descendants stand before the court today as people entitled to the protection of English law.

---

[71] M. de Vattel, *The Law of Nations or Principles of the Law of Nature Applied to the Conduct and Affairs of Nations and Sovereigns: A Work Tending to Display the True Interest of Powers* (Dublin: Luke White, 1792), p. 164. Translated from the French.

The attorney general would be caught in a catch-22 situation. If he maintained that the indigenous people were not sovereign people, then the East India Company's Act of State trick, which denied access to the courts by sovereign people who were parties to a treaty with the sovereign state of the British government, couldn't be invoked. Alternatively, if the attorney general conceded the sovereignty of the indigenous people in order to invoke the discredited Act of State doctrine, the indigenous people would say, "Thanks. That is what we have been claiming since 1788."

If the High Court not only agreed that the late Mr Coe had the right to have his case heard but then had to deal with his argument, they may wish that the government at the time had taken up the offer of the indigenous people at Uluru in 2017.

> Our Aboriginal and Torres Strait Islander tribes were the first sovereign Nations of the Australian continent and its adjacent islands and possessed it under our own laws and customs. This our ancestors did, according to the reckoning of our culture, from the Creation, according to the common law from "time immemorial," and according to science more than 60,000 years ago.
>
> This sovereignty is a spiritual notion: the ancestral tie between the land, or "mother nature," and the Aboriginal and Torres Strait Islander peoples who were born therefrom, remain attached thereto, and must one day return thither to be united

with our ancestors. This link is the basis
of the ownership of the soil, or better,
of sovereignty. It has never been ceded
or extinguished, and co-exists with the
sovereignty of the Crown.

How could it be otherwise? That peoples
possessed a land for sixty millennia and this
sacred link disappears from world history in
merely the last two hundred years? [72]

I should admit to being a run-of-the-mill lawyer, but even so, I find that there is robust legal support for the claim of sovereignty in this statement but also a concession to the new imperatives facing our two nations. If the new Mr Coe could get to the High Court and persuade it to follow the law, there would be no need for an alteration in our Constitution as its security would be in doubt.

A new challenge to sovereignty could not be lightly dismissed. If the High Court is still disposed to deny the indigenous people the right to bring their challenge in an Australian court, it would be necessary to explain how the cases on which Gibbs and Brennan relied supported a refusal of the right of the indigenous people to prosecute their challenge in an Australian court. Perhaps they could rely on the decision of the Privy Council in the case where the East India Company welched on the agreement to pay the nawab a pension for life. But the basis for the decision in that case was that the deal was, in fact, a treaty between two sovereign people that made it an Act of State, which prevented the

---

[72] See https://ulurustatement.org/the-statement.

beneficiaries of the nawab's estate from seeking recovery of the pension. Apart from the daylight robbery cases, all the other decisions of the Privy Council have relied on the proposition that the nawabs who sued and the East India Company were two separate sovereign peoples. Being an action between two sovereign people, the court decided that it had no authority to hear the action and, therefore, dismissed the claims of the local Indian nawabs or their relatives. For the High Court to pull the Act of State out of their box of tricks to deny the indigenous people the right to challenge sovereignty and dispossession, the High Court would have to find as fact that the indigenous people were sovereign peoples. That is precisely what Mr Coe claimed in his case, which Gibbs dismissed out of hand.

13

The Deck is Stacked Against the Indigenous People

The refusal of the High Court to permit the indigenous people to challenge the validity of the proclamation of sovereignty by Captain Cook secured for the newcomers the suspicious legality of the indigenous people surrendering their land to the Crown and subjecting themselves to its law. As a result, the indigenous people were reduced to beggar status in their attempts to salvage what is left of this land.

In a real sense, the High Court is conflicted. If it faced the reality that no magic can confer jurisprudential legality on the unilateral act of Captain Cook proclaiming this land for his king, the entire underpinning of our modern society would be in jeopardy. In this environment, the High Court becomes the protector of our institutions, persuaded by practical considerations rather than legal principles. The discredited Act of State doctrine stands as a frail legal fig leaf and prevents a profound disruption of Australian society. Perhaps that is a good thing. But it does nothing to assuage the descendants of those who occupied and cared for this country for over forty thousand years. Some recognition has been given to this dilemma. Judge McHugh, in a revelatory moment, summarised the plight of the indigenous people:

The dispossession of the Aboriginal peoples from their lands was a great wrong. Many people believe that those of us who are the beneficiaries of that wrong have a moral responsibility to redress it to the extent that it can be redressed. But it is becoming increasingly clear—to me, at all events— that redress cannot be achieved by a system that depends on evaluating the competing legal rights of landholders and native-title holders. The deck is stacked against the native-title holders whose fragile rights must give way to the superior rights of the landholders whenever the two classes of rights conflict.[73]

Despite this and other occasional passages of insight into the plight of the original inhabitants of this country, The High Court continues to be the High Priest protecting the establishment.

For many years, the South Australian government wanted to build a bridge to Hindmarsh Island in South Australia. The project was delayed by repetitive attempts by a group of Aboriginal women who claimed that the building of a bridge would infringe beliefs that were secret to them. One of the delays involved a prolonged constitutional issue over the appointment of a federal judge to conduct an inquiry into the legitimacy of the women's claims. That case resulted in the High Court ruling against the appointment of the judge.

---

[73] Western Australia v Ward [2002] HCA 28 at page 222.

In an act of frustration at the years of delay and irritating legal opposition, which some believed had no merit, the federal government stepped in and passed an act of Parliament, preventing the women from further delaying the building of the bridge. Rather than accelerating the construction of the bridge, it resulted in the women taking further legal action by challenging the validity of the federal legislation.

It is a messy story involving some constitutional history and the ingenuity of our High Court judges to give novel meanings to words. The Constitution confers on Parliament powers to pass certain laws. If it attempts to pass laws beyond those powers, the High Court can strike down the laws as invalid in that they are said to be beyond power.

You might recall that prior to 1967, the existence of the Aboriginal people was not recognised in our Constitution. But after a referendum, the Constitution was altered. Before 1967, section 51 of the Constitution said:

> The Parliament shall, subject to this Constitution, have power to make laws for the peace, order and good government of the Commonwealth in relation to
>
> (xxvi} the people of any race, other than the aboriginal race in any State, for whom it is deemed necessary to make special laws.

After the 1967 referendum, the words, "other than the aboriginal race," were omitted. As a result, the Parliament had power to make laws for all races, including the aboriginal race, for whom it is deemed necessary.

On the face of it, my reading of the section suggests that it was not intended to give the Parliament power to punish the indigenous people or to deprive them of any of their rights. I am sure that if it was suggested during the run up to the referendum that it was intended for the alteration of the Constitution to give Parliament power to punish the Aboriginal people or deprive them of their rights, it would never have been adopted by the Australian people. By the time the Aboriginal women from Hindmarsh Island got to the High Court, the judges had a different slant on the section.

In 1995, the Aboriginal women made application to the minister pursuant to the Aboriginal and Torres Strait Islander Heritage Protection Act 1984 (Cth) for a declaration that Hindmarsh Island was a protected area. If the minister made the declaration, it would prevent any construction work, such as a bridge, taking place in the area.

In 1997, Parliament passed the Hindmarsh Island Bridge Act 1997, which prohibited the minister from making a declaration protecting Hindmarsh Island, and specifically from a declaration that would prevent the construction of a bridge. The effect of this legislation was to stop the women from obtaining a declaration under the Heritage Protection Act that would have the effect of preventing the bridge construction. This was intended to stop the objection to the bridge in its tracks. But the legislation was in fact denying the Aboriginal people the right to seek a declaration protecting a heritage area. One act of Parliament gave the Aboriginal people a right, and the other act took it away.

The Aboriginal people cried foul and appealed to the High Court for a declaration that the Bridge Act was invalid.[74] Their argument was that the Bridge Act effectively deprived them of their rights to seek a declaration protecting a sacred site. The only power Parliament had under the Constitution in relation to Aborigines was section 51 (xxvi). They argued that it was never intended for that section to be used to pass a law in respect of Aborigines, which had the effect of punishing them or depriving them of their rights. Quite the contrary. The Constitution enabled Parliament to make laws for the Aborigines that it, "deemed necessary." No stretch of imagination or legal gymnastics could possibly result in these words being interpreted to mean that depriving the Aboriginal people of their statutory rights could be deemed necessary for them.

By now, the Aboriginal people should have been satisfied with the crumbs fed to them in Mabo and saved their money. The majority of the judges in an endless journey into the highways and byways of legal precedent didn't buy the argument and concluded that it was within Parliament's power to take away Aboriginal rights.

In a similarly lengthy judgement laced with refences to other cases, Judge Kirby came to the opposite conclusion. One of the areas of history that interested him was the debate leading to the 1967 amendment. In traversing the records of those debates, there was not the slightest suggestion that the amendment could result in the diminution of the rights of the Aboriginal people. According to Kirby, it was quite the contrary. The whole thrust of the movement to amend

---

[74] Kartenyeri v. The Commonwealth (1998) HCA 22.

the Constitution was to enable Parliament to make laws for the benefit of the Aboriginal people.

This is how he summarised the situation:

> The Bridge Act does not answer to the description of a law with respect to the people of any race for whom it is deemed necessary to make special laws. It is a special law; that is true. But it is detrimental to, and adversely discriminatory against, people of the Aboriginal race of Australia by reference to their race. As such it falls outside the class of laws which the race power in the Australian Constitution permits. No other head of power being propounded to support the validity of the Bridge Act, it is wholly unconstitutional.[75]

To arrive at their various decisions, the judgement occupied over fifty pages, and there were 350 references to other cases and authorities. Judge McHugh was one of the judges who found against the Aborigines, and five years later, was to declare that the deck was stacked against the indigenous people, perhaps reflecting that he had played a part in dealing their hand.

An issue that was not argued in this case was the purpose of the legislation. The obvious purpose of the legislation was to enable a bridge to be built in South Australia. The Constitution conferred no such power on Parliament. The

---

[75] Ibid.

building of bridges in South Australia was the domain of the South Australian Parliament. Perhaps the lawyers missed something.

When you get to the High Court, the *Oxford Dictionary* is of little help in understanding the meaning of words.

14

The Stolen Generation

The intersection of the indigenous people with the British and Australian legal systems has been disastrous for the Aboriginal people of this country. Until 1968, the only indigenous people who saw the inside of our courts were people accused of crimes. The evidence of their lack of success in the Australian justice system is demonstrated by the huge disparity between the percentage of Aborigines incarcerated in our prison system and their percentage of the overall Australian population. That is not to mention the frequency of their deaths in custody as against those of white people.

These disgraceful phenomena occasionally arouse some cosmetic concern manifesting in a Royal commission inquiring into Aboriginal deaths in custody, or more recently, an intervention because of allegations that paedophilia was rife in Aboriginal communities. It is sad that there was not a similar response to the conduct of the Catholic Church.

In the end, nothing happens, but for the moment, the establishment's conscience is salved because it has at least done something.

The one question that is not seriously asked when confronted with this institutionalised dysfunction is, "What is the basic cause of the problem?" Every now and then, the government thinks it knows how to fix it, but its persistent failure compels the response that it doesn't. One reason for this is that the non-indigenous population has been here for two hundred years, but the Aborigines have been here for over forty thousand years. For more than 150 years since 1788, the majority of the non-indigenous people of this country had not the slightest awareness of the rich and ancient history of the original inhabitants. It is unlikely that in the short history of Western occupation of this country, we, as newcomers, could gain more than a glimpse of the tens of thousands of years of history that preceded the arrival of the First Fleet. Accordingly, public policy towards the indigenous people is often developed based on ignorant assumptions.

It is inconceivable that in those few moments of combative engagement with the original inhabitants of this country, we, as a continuum of the early arrivals to this country since 1788, could aspire to having the slightest insight or understanding of the culture of the ancient civilisation that then existed. Burdened by this incomprehensible ignorance, the conceit in believing that modern non indigenous society knows what is best for these people is stupefying.

In recent times there have been extensive demonstrations about the plight of black people generally, and here in Australia, about the plight of the indigenous people. Once again, the demonstrations have activated the established political system to come up with cosmetic solutions that will not arrest the dysfunction between indigenous aspirations and the world view of our political establishment.

The failure of our legal system to understand the amplitude of this chasm has resulted in the almost total rejection of the Aboriginal plea for recognition. Our legal system demanded that the Aboriginal people talk in the language of the law inherited from England. The indigenous people are forced to redefine their belief system so that it harmonises with Australian law. This incongruous expectation was destined to be a rejection of the Aboriginal voice. I wonder if Judge Brennan ever pondered the profound depth of the insult to the descendants of the original inhabitants of this land when he told them their rights had been washed away by the tide of history?

> We have occupied and cared for the land of this country which is the source of our spiritual energy and our spiritual resting place and you have taken it from us. You tell us that your English law has washed it away. Nothing can wash it away; it is now being desecrated and we no longer have ties to our spiritual home.

Such an argument would not prevail in our legal system.

The expectation that the indigenous people have to constrain their pleas for recognition of their rights within the language of our common law creates all the failures that arise from translation. The difference between the Aboriginal world view and that of Western society is culturally chasmic. Our legal system is insensitive to this divide and insists that it be ignored when the indigenous people seek relief in our court system.

In recent times, attempts have been made to reconstruct history. There is a view that much good came out of the process of taking Aboriginal children from their parents and placing them in institutions, where they would be "saved." There is no doubt that there is a grain, but only a grain of truth in that proposition.

Josephine Flood, an archaeologist who has made a great contribution to Aboriginal history while condemning some excesses of the programme, nevertheless reserves her criticism for the commission that heard evidence and issued a report on the episode.[76] It may well be that the commission's report, *Bringing Them Home*, was tarnished with bias and did not alter the fact that a policy that resulted in the most horrific dislocation of Aboriginal family life was condoned by the High Court. The extent to which the stolen generation issue has been politicised in this country is disgraceful.

In the late fifties and early sixties of the last century, I was a young lawyer working with the Northern Territory Administration in Darwin. The phrase that was on everyone's lips was, "We have to assimilate the Aborigines." However, the fine print rarely saw the light of day. The driving policy of assimilation was to achieve a de facto eugenic mutation of the Aboriginal race. Let me come back to that.

My first experience of assimilation occurred when I had a call from the associate to Judge Kriewaldt of the Northern Territory Supreme Court. I was invited to meet the judge.

---

[76] Josephine Flood, *The Original Australians* (A & U, 2019), pp. 276–286.

When I walked into his chambers, I was immediately aware of photographs of the judge sitting amongst Aboriginal elders. After introductions, he learnt that I had come from Canberra, where a famous lawyer by the name of John Fleming was dean of the law school.[77] The judge then posed this problem for me to discuss with Fleming when next in Canberra.

> Coutts, I have just completed a murder trial, an Aboriginal man. He was a member of a clan of Aborigines when a member raped the wife of another member of the clan. The person was hauled up before the elders because of the rape. The elders found him guilty according to Aboriginal law and sentenced him to death. They appointed a member of the clan to carry out the execution, which he did. The person who carried out the execution was the Aborigine who came before me charged with murder according to our law. Coutts, ask your academic mate Fleming how he would have handled the matter.

That was my introduction to the practical consequences of assimilation. The Aborigine was no longer allowed to practice indigenous law. Even in those days, not knowing much about Aboriginal history, I was disturbed. It seemed to me that we were telling the indigenous people that we

---

[77] John Fleming's book on torts, written from 1957 to 1960, is now in its tenth edition. It is used in all English-speaking jurisdictions. Without Professor Fleming's help, I may never have graduated in law.

knew what was best for them. Even if we didn't—and we didn't—they just had to face the reality that their days were over, and they had to adjust to our laws. The experience that day has lived with me to this day.

Another experience I had when working in Darwin involved a meeting with a famous Territorian, Tiger Brennan, who was a member of the local legislative council. He came to my office one day and told me this story.

"It's a bit of a joke, Coutts, although it is not funny. Down the track on the holdings, where Aborigines hang out, the station managers have cans of methylated spirits that they keep locked. Do you know what happens on pension days, Coutts?"

I admitted that I had no idea about what happened on pension days. "Mysteriously, the methylated spirits can become unlocked, and many of the Aborigines drink the stuff. Do you know what happens then, Coutts?" Once again, I admitted my ignorance. "There is a freight train that occasionally travels from Adelaide River to Darwin. Well, after drinking metho, some of these Aborigines decide that they are going to walk to the big smoke.[78] You can guess what happens if a freight train comes along. They just collect the bodies and move them off the track."

I was horrified. We were corrupting the indigenous people and then holding them to account for breaking our laws. I was appalled at this idea of so-called assimilation.

---

[78] That was a term commonly used in those days by people down the track to describe Darwin.

It was not until many years later that I learned of the extent of the policy and its evil justification. This is an extract from a debate in the New South Wales Parliament. The following are two quotations by members of the New South Wales Parliament on the introduction of the Aborigines Protection Act 1915:

> It is not a question of stealing the children, but of saving them … I am sorry to say that, generally speaking, the rising generation of these people are mostly half castes; very few full bloods are left, and the half casts remain in the camp to be brought down to the same standard as the aborigines … if we give the board the powers, I am seeking to bestow under this amending bill … the aborigines will soon become a negligible quantity and the young people will merge into present civilisation and become worthy citizens.[79]

> There is a very fervent and strong affection between the parents and relations and these half cast and other children—an affection quite as strong as that which exists amongst any of the white population (NSWPD 1915 page 1355 link up page 62).

But he went on to say, "There is only one way to do this thing … the Board must have the authority to have the powers given under this Bill … The race is rapidly dying

---

[79] *(Due to the author Louis Coutts' illness, full details can't be provided)*

out, and there will be no occasions for these camps in the future."[80]

People can say what they like about the stolen generation, and it would be a complete catastrophe if some good didn't come out of it. However, the purpose of taking children from their parents had nothing to do with their welfare. The purpose was to eliminate the Aboriginal race, and the programme continued into the 1970s, when we were shocked at what was happening in South Africa.

Shortly after the decision in Mabo's case, there was a slight reprieve for the Wik people in Queensland. In that case, the High Court found that native title could co-exist with occupation pursuant to a pastoral lease. Later legislation would tighten the rules, but in the meantime, the indigenous people were buoyed by the limited success they had obtained in the High Court. Almost at the same time of the Wik case, and emboldened by the limited success in Mabo, some of the casualties of the stolen generation sued the Commonwealth government in the case of Kruger v. The Commonwealth.[81]

I can't dwell on this case as I find it too disturbing. But it did help me to gain a little insight into the difficulty of the Aboriginal people seeking justice in our courts. The discovery was so obvious that I am embarrassed to admit my stupidity. Before I make the confession, it is necessary to tell you a little about the case.

Section 122 of the Constitution empowered Parliament to make laws for the government of the territories. This

---

[80] *(Due to the author Louis Coutts' illness, full details can't be provided)*
[81] Kruger v. The Commonwealth (1997) CLR 190.

enabled the Northern Territory Legislative Council to pass the Aboriginal's Ordinance in 1918. This ordinance empowered the protector of Aborigines to remove Aborigines and "half-castes" from their families and place them in reserves. In other words, it was the stolen generation law. The argument of the indigenous people was that section 122 of the Constitution did not empower Parliament to make laws that enabled the Northern Territory Legislative Council to discriminate against the Aborigines because of their religion. They also argued that what happened as a result of this legislation was genocide.

This is where I suddenly saw the light. The judges on the High Court had a field day indulging themselves in academic research and putting it together in language that few could understand. To them it was a wonderful intellectual exercise. And, of course, they dismissed the claim and ordered the Aboriginal people to pay the costs. I know that the law has to be guided by principle and not emotions, but that doesn't prohibit an understanding of the sensitivities involved in a case. If a party is morally aggrieved, even though there might be no remedy in law for that grievance, there is nothing to prevent judges from expressing their understanding of the moral harm suffered by a party. In this case, there was no such sensitivity, and the arguments of the Aboriginal people were dismissed with the frequent and too familiar arcane language that disinfected the process. But it was one passage that really struck me and awakened me to my stupidity in not understanding the dysfunctional relationship between Aborigines issues and our legal process.

Judge Dawson made the following observation:

> The measures contemplated by the
> legislation of which the Plaintiffs complain
> would appear to be ill-advised or mistaken,
> particularly by contemporary standards.
> However, a shift in view of the justice or
> morality of those measures taken under the
> Ordinance which was repealed over forty
> years ago does not of itself point to the
> constitutional invalidity of that legislation
> and it is to the legal basis of the Plaintiffs'
> claims that I now must turn.[82]

Dawson was speaking one language, which is the language of our own legal system. The Aborigines were speaking another language, which was a product of their ancient adaptation to this land; a language understood by those who inherited the traditions that have evolved over tens of thousands of years and have become part of their culture. If it is a language that the judges of the High Court can understand, there is no evidence to suggest that they have learnt that language. The pronouncements of the courts of this country in major indigenous litigation are conducted exclusively in the arcane language of the law.

For the first 150 years of the occupation of this land by Western society, most of the non-indigenous people of this country were totally unaware of the existence of indigenous culture. Certainly, in the few years preceding the indigenous appearances in our courts as supplicants, our law has not,

---

[82] Kruger v. The Commonwealth, ibid., p. 52.

and probably cannot bridge that gap or understand the language with which the indigenous people want to speak.

Dawson seemed to be arguing that what was done in 1918 was only ill-advised according to our contemporary standards but was OK in 1918 by our standards. From the stories I have read about the taking of children from their parents as a result of this law, it is clear that the policy and conduct were hated and deeply resented by the Aboriginal people. Dawson, together with his fellow judges, was unable to see things other than from the perspective of his own experience and our language. If it had been possible to talk with a mother in 1918 who had her child stolen from her, I can't imagine the grief and sorrow she would have expressed. By her standards in 1918, to describe what was being done as ill-advised would have affronted the mother. According to her standards, for mothers who had their children taken from them, what was being done was heartbreakingly horrible. This passage of Dawson exposed a terrible weakness in our legal system that requires the indigenous people to transpose English and Australian constitutional law to indigenous circumstances, which is an impossibility. At least one High Court judge has admitted as such.[83]

This inability to see the indigenous perspective is systemic in the prevailing culture of Australian society. The Aboriginal people have developed a different way of thinking. To suggest that after a couple hundred years of violent interaction with these people it is possible for the political and legal establishment of this country to righteously determine what

---

[83] See the statement of Judge McHugh in Ward v. The Commonwealth (2002) CLR 1 at page. *(Due to the author Louis Coutts' illness, full details can't be provided)*

is good for them reflects such a regressive state of maturity that disqualifies the establishment from interfering with their affairs.

And yet, the damage is done. Aboriginal youths are being locked up by the day in numbers that are so disproportionate to their membership in our society. That compels the conclusion that the formal political establishment, and not the aboriginal people, have much to learn and a long way to go in bridging this gap of misunderstanding.

A starting point seems to me to be an acceptance that this non-indigenous political and legal establishment does not have the skills to communicate with the Aboriginal people as they intersect with our law. As more and more of the unwanted citizens of Britain were poured into this country, together with their gaolers, the process of corruption of Aboriginal culture commenced, and it continues. The evidence has been recorded in the transcripts of the Yolngu people's case and the stolen generation case. Before the arrival of the convicts, the Aboriginal people had lived in peace with this land and cared for it since the Dreamtime and creation.

Having corrupted these people, we now hold them to account to Australian laws without having the faintest idea of the harm such a regime is still causing. The next step is to admit that the non-indigenous establishment has no idea how to fix the problem. To the extent that it continues to maintain that it knows what to do, such as with the disastrous intervention policy when false stories were circulated about the extent of paedophilia and alcohol abuse, monumental mistakes continue to be made.

The stolen generation case was a wonderful opportunity in the history of Australian jurisprudence for the legal establishment to put its hands up and admit that according to Aboriginal standards at the time, what was done was inexcusable. To submit indigenous grievances to determination by English and Australian laws, which were the cause of the problem, and our courts, which are not adjusted to understanding the indigenous narrative, perpetuates the chasm between the indigenous people and our law, and ensures the continuity of the disasters that are constantly inflicted upon the descendants of the original inhabitants.

We will see in the next chapter how the concept of jurisprudence sometimes has a part to play in our law when confronted with new social phenomena. But sadly, it is a concept to which our High Court turns a blind eye.

While not directly connected to the stolen generation issue, the High Court had another opportunity to address the imbalance of our treatment of Aboriginal criminality. In a case in which an Aboriginal person in the remand centre in Broken Hill seriously injured a warder, he was sentenced by the trial judge to a non-parole period of four years. The Crown appealed the sentence on the basis that it was inadequate. The person's background was summarised by six of the judges of the High Court who subscribed to the one opinion:

> The appellant is an Aboriginal man who was raised in Wilcannia, a town in far-western New South Wales. He is one of a number of siblings. He grew up in a

household in which alcohol abuse and violence were commonplace. He has had little formal education and is unable to read or write. He started drinking alcohol and taking prohibited drugs when he was 13 years old. He reports having witnessed his father stabbing his mother 15 times. He and his siblings all have records for violence. The appellant's record of juvenile offending commenced when he was 12 years old. From that age he was regularly detained in juvenile detention centres. When he turned 18 he was transferred to an adult prison. He has a long record of convictions including for offences of violence. He was 29 years old at the date of the present offences. He has spent much of his adult life in prison. He gives a history of repeated suicide attempts. He has maintained a long-term relationship with a woman by whom he has a daughter. He and his partner are both alcoholics. The child has been placed in the care of her maternal grandmother.[84]

The judges upheld the Crown's appeal and increased the sentence to a non-parole period of five years. In doing so, the judges made the following observation: "An Aboriginal offender's deprived background may mitigate the sentence that would otherwise be appropriate for the offence in the

---

[84] *(Due to the author Louis Coutts' illness, full details can't be provided)*

same way that the deprived background of a non-Aboriginal offender may mitigate that offender's sentence."[85]

It is incomprehensible that the background of an Aboriginal person whose people have been cast adrift from their cultural heritage and forced to accommodate to an environment totally foreign to their traditions can be compared with the background of people born into our Western traditions. It is another example of the chasm in language that is so apparent when Aboriginal people intersect with our justice system, either as a supplicant or a sufferer.

---

[85] Bugmy v. R (2013)302ALR192.

15

Forgiveness

Since the abandonment of the white Australia policy, Australia has increasingly become a multicultural society with migrants of diverse ethnic backgrounds having to accommodate to the political and legal institutions of this country that had their commencement in 1788. Australian society recognises the rights of individuals from different backgrounds and different beliefs to continue those practices and beliefs provided they are not inconsistent with our laws. They become a part of the continuum of our modern society. But no such accommodation has been extended to the descendants of the original inhabitants of this country.

I am sure that anthropologists and specialists in comparative religion would be able to demonstrate all the differences between Aboriginal spirituality and that of other religions and beliefs. But there is one difference in particular that is especially relevant when considering the current state of Aboriginality in Australia. Aboriginal spirituality is intimately connected with the land, which is no longer their own. I am sure that is what Judge McHugh had in mind in the famous passage in which he said that the deck was stacked against the Aboriginal people. I quoted part of that passage in the previous chapter, and forgive me for repeating it here by quoting it in full:

> The dispossession of the Aboriginal peoples from their lands was a great wrong. Many people believe that those of us who are the beneficiaries of that wrong have a moral responsibility to redress it to the extent that it can be redressed. But it is becoming increasingly clear—to me, at all events—that redress cannot be achieved by a system that depends on evaluating the competing legal rights of landholders and native-title holders. The deck is stacked against the native-title holders whose fragile rights must give way to the superior rights of the landholders whenever the two classes of rights conflict. And it is a system that is costly and time-consuming. At present the chief beneficiaries of the system are the legal representatives of the parties. It may be that the time has come to think of abandoning the present system, a system that simply seeks to declare and enforce the legal rights of the parties, irrespective of their merits. A better system may be an arbitral system that declares what the rights of the parties ought to be according to the justice and circumstances of the individual case. Implementing such a system in the federal sphere may have constitutional

difficulties but may not be impossible. At all events, it is worth considering.[86]

It is the first sentence that identifies the problem. The dispossession of the Aboriginal people from their lands has resulted in them being denied access to their spiritual home. Not any of the various religions or spiritual beliefs of the newcomers to this country since 1788 have been centred around land. It has been easy for the believers in different religions to transport their beliefs and religions with them. One of the central features of Aboriginal spirituality was the totemic infrastructure that had criss-crossed the land since the Dreaming and creation. With dispossession, this has been destroyed, and the descendants of the original inhabitants are now expected to be part of this continuum of Western society and forever accept the consequences of the tide of history and forsake their religion. To the extent that there remain some holy sites, the indigenous people have to navigate a 558-page set of rules established by the Australian Parliament.

Today's Aborigine who wants to cling to the ancient traditions of his or her forebears is caught between clinging to those ancient beliefs without contact with the land of which they are an intimate part and being part of our Western society in order to survive. In a real sense, they have been deprived of the opportunity to practice their spirituality. Many of the consequences are obvious, such as the disproportionate percentage of indigenous people in prisons coupled with an atrocious statistic of deaths in custody.

---

[86] Ward v. The Commonwealth (2002) CLR 1 at page. *(Due to the author Louis Coutts' illness, full details can't be provided)*

A closer inspection of the observation of Judge McHugh's writing is enlightening. It is one of the few passages in which a student of Australian law will find a reference to justice in a report of cases in our law reports. It is so sad that a judge of the High Court of Australia is compelled to reflect that justice is inaccessible to the indigenous people because the law is more concerned with the rights of the newcomer.

McHugh's reflection could be interpreted as an admission that the High Court is no longer able to do its job because it, "seeks to declare the legal rights of the parties, irrespective of their merits." We have seen many examples of the consequences of this approach in the many stories contained in this book. However, it is particularly sad that the barriers to justice for the Aboriginal people are impenetrable and that the High Court is the instrument perpetuating this disadvantage. It is a sign of a wider problem with the court.

The doctrine of precedent has become a whipping boy. Terms such as "justice," "jurisprudence," "rule of law," and "fairness" rarely appear in judgements emanating from the High Court. Indeed, there is a reticence to do so because these concepts sit uneasily with the doctrine of precedent. If a court's function is to administer justice, there would be an outcry because the term is so loose. Uncertainty about the law would result, or so its critics say. But when we consider the extent of disagreement between the judges and throughout the court system, it is fair to ask whether the current model for deciding cases is working. More importantly, does it have the confidence of the community? In so far as McHugh is concerned, it is certainly not working, and the indigenous people are paying the price.

There is also the temptation to think that the judges of the High Court have an unconscious bias when it comes to indigenous issues. The argument of Mr Coe that the proclamation of sovereignty over this county by Captain Cook and Captain Philip was invalid was met with disdain, rather than with a reasoned analysis of the doctrine of Act of State. It was such a convenient tool to stop the argument in its tracks. Nothing can be more effective than a judge telling a party that he or she does not have the right to have their complaint entertained by a court. It avoids the necessity of having to deal with the argument. However, when the argument is of such profound importance as to challenge the validity of the institutions of government of this country, the temptation to suspect that it is an argument the court really doesn't want to see the light of day in a courtroom in this country is not easily dismissed. As I pointed out in discussing the case of Mabo, there is a touch of hypocrisy in the approach of the court because in that case, the court did permit the indigenous people to challenge an Act of State.

The result of the monumental court challenges to dispossession of both their land and their children has been less than poor for the indigenous people. The decision of the High Court in the Mabo case is hailed as a great breakthrough in the aspirations of the indigenous people. In reality, it put paid to their aspiration of challenging the validity of the annexation of their country. The result of Mabo was to legitimise the dispossession. It was followed by the massive codification of the legal maze that the indigenous people had to navigate in order to establish a right to their own land. Once having navigated this maze, the result is often a dead end and a costly defeat for the Aboriginal people. However, it did give the lawyers the opportunity to indulge in the process of creating thousands of pages of esoteric legal dissertations that have shored up the barricades to indigenous justice.

The most glaring example of the intellectual indifference to the feelings of the Aboriginal people must have been the decision of the High Court in the Hindmarsh Bridge case, which we discussed earlier. You might remember that in that case, Parliament passed an act denying the right of the Aboriginal women to seek protection of a native heritage site despite the fact that another act of Parliament conferred upon them such a right. The Aboriginal women argued that the amendment to the Constitution that empowered Parliament to make laws for the Aboriginal people did not confer on Parliament powers to make laws for their disadvantage. But the majority of judges on the High Court said that was precisely what the amendment to the Constitution permitted and proceeded to deny the Aboriginal women their rights.

When confronted with situations that occurred in different times, the High Court tends to ask itself, "What was the law when that incident occurred?" For example, in the case where a woman complained of being raped by her husband in 1963, the High Court in 2004 applied itself to determining whether or not in 1963 a so-called precedent from 1674 granted a husband an immunity against prosecution for the rape of his wife. In the stolen generation case, the High Court questioned whether laws of 1918 were offensive to community standards in those days and decided that they were not. In the two indigenous cases that either questioned or touched on the legality of British sovereignty and annexation of the land, the High Court has not asked itself whether such conduct was in accordance with the law at the time. Indeed, relying on dubious precedent, the court refuses the indigenous people the right to raise the argument in an Australian court. It has slammed the door in the face of the indigenous people by determining that the question of the legality of the proclamation of sovereignty over and the annexation of this land is off limits and cannot be argued in our courts.

The result has been the creation of an artificial relationship between the newcomers and the descendants of the ancient people who originally occupied this country. Following the decision in the case of Mabo v. The State of Queensland, an act of Parliament—the Native Titles Act—has become law. It contains 253 sections plus schedules and occupies 558 pages. This horrendous document, which defines the relationship between "us" as the descendants of the European settlers and the indigenous people, is an act of parliament that does not represent the indigenous people. Apart from informal bodies that have no effective representative capacities, the indigenous people have to speak through the language of the laws of Australia as contained in a grotesquely massive piece of legislation that solidifies the tenure of the beneficiaries of the grants of Aboriginal land to the newcomers to this country. To the extent that the legislation and the ruling of the High Court creates a pathway for the indigenous people to reclaim what is left of their land, they have to negotiate an expensive journey through the eye of a needle.

Faced with the reality of dispossession and the unassailable legal and practical control that the government has over this land and its people, it is inconceivable that anger does not lie in the hearts of many of the descendants of the original inhabitants. To make a claim for their land, besides having to find their way through the missive of unintelligible legislation, they then need the resources to meet the formidable obstacle of the judges of our High Court. This legal and legislative roadblock sends a message to the indigenous people that their day is done, and in the future, only the crumbs that are left will fall from the rich man's table.

Without any hope of challenging the legality of sovereignty, without any hope of turning back the tide of dispossession, and with the diminishing links to their own origins and spirituality, it is difficult to see what is still on the table for the Aboriginal people.

Despite their modest success in the case of Mabo and, to a certain extent, in the case of the Wik people, the structural boundaries that confine and limit the options of the Aboriginal people are impenetrable. The result is not so much issues such as the disproportionate incarceration of their people and their dependence on the handouts from the government of the day. It is perhaps presumptuous of me to suspect that the greater damage is the severance from their traditions, the loss of their culture, the disappearance of their language, and the fading away of their narratives. In turn, these tragedies flow from our inability to speak and understand their language with a correlative expectation that they speak and understand the language of our Western institutions, particularly the language of our legal system.

Facing this huge edifice of Western institutions with which they only have a brief familiarity, and with a yearning to remain in touch with their ancient traditions, solace can only be extended to these people with an acceptance that the legal foundation for the constitutional structure of this country is insecure.

In the face of the awful damage inflicted on these people and their ancestors, more than words are necessary to secure their acceptance of the new regime in which they are captives. At the moment, I suspect the prevailing political view is that the Aboriginal people have to accept the status quo.

That, of course, was the message of Judge Brennan in the Mabo case: "indigenous rights have been washed away by the tide of history." In the stolen generation case, Judge Dawson expressed the view that what was done in 1918, while perhaps offensive to our modern values, was not offensive in the days of removing Aboriginal children from their parents to civilise them. To the extent that the immorality of the exercise is now accepted, the contemporary understanding of society is that it was all fixed when the prime minister stood up in the house of Parliament and said, "Sorry," as though that was another act in wiping away the tide of history. The apology solved nothing.

Since 1788, the prevailing view of the various institutions of government of this country can be described as patronizing: "We know what is best for the Aboriginal people; to the extent that there are problems, we know how to fix them." The sad history of the so-called fixes is compelling evidence that "we" don't know how to fix the problems.

The Aboriginal people are grieving over the destruction of their ancient civilisation and look hopelessly at the mess, knowing there is little that can be done to restore what has been lost. Our legal system provides them with no solace. It is necessary to bridge that gap if only slightly.

Instead of lying to the Aboriginal people and telling them that we know how to fix their problems, there must be an acknowledgement that the problems of the Aboriginal people are enduring. We can ask the indigenous people, even at this late hour in their distress, "What do you want us, the newcomers to this country, to do so that you can accept us? Tell us what acts of contrition are necessary so that we can live in greater harmony with you." Perhaps they might say, "Until you accept that we have never surrendered sovereignty over this county and that we are still a sovereign people, we can't start to bridge the gap. But once we get over that hurdle, we will put a stop to our people being imprisoned in your gaols and have our own prison system."

They might say, "Just accept that the English invaded our country, and there is no legal justification for the proclamation of sovereignty or the annexation of our land. After all, you are the newcomers, and you have never asked permission to occupy this land." I don't know, but I imagine that there would be many items on the wish list before there can be forgiveness.

Judge McHugh put it succinctly when he said, "Many people believe that those of us who are the beneficiaries of that wrong have a moral responsibility to redress it to the extent that it can be redressed." I see that observation made by a judge of the highest court in this land as an invitation to the indigenous people to tell us, "the beneficiaries of the wrongs," what we can do to redress the wrongs to the extent they can be redressed.

An apology is one thing, but forgiveness is another. And so far, we as "beneficiaries of the wrong" have not sought forgiveness. Indeed, I suspect that there are many in the community who still cling to a construction of our history in which the newcomers are not beneficiaries of wrongs to the indigenous people. But McHugh, in his official capacity as a judge of the High Court, has condensed the argument into accepting the undeniable fact of dispossession.

The time has come to introduce into the narrative of Australian law another narrative: the narrative of the indigenous people. Perhaps then our nation can move forward from forgiveness to some compassionate process that can never amend the wrong that has been done but may bring about a harmony in the relationship between the new and the ancient inhabitants of this country.

In May 2017, a major conference was held in the shadows of the Aboriginal spiritual symbol of Uluru in the Northern Territory. It was a conference seeking a way forward and resulted in the adoption by the descendants of the original inhabitants of this country of a statement "of the Heart." Following are the introductory paragraphs of that statement:

> Our Aboriginal and Torres Strait Islander tribes were the first sovereign Nations of the Australian continent and its adjacent islands, and possessed it under our own laws and customs. This our ancestors did, according to the reckoning of our culture, from the Creation, according to the common law from 'time immemorial',

and according to science more than 60,000 years ago.

This sovereignty is a spiritual notion: the ancestral tie between the land, or 'mother nature', and the Aboriginal and Torres Strait Islander peoples who were born therefrom, remain attached thereto, and must one day return thither to be united with our ancestors. This link is the basis of the ownership of the soil, or better, of sovereignty. It has never been ceded or extinguished, and co-exists with the sovereignty of the Crown.

How could it be otherwise? That peoples possessed a land for sixty millennia and this sacred link disappears from world history in merely the last two hundred years?

16

Precedent and Justice

I have made occasional references to the doctrine of precedent, which is intended as a tool to secure an element of certainty in our law. Lower courts are bound by the decisions of higher courts with the result that once a decision is made by our High Court on a particular point of law, it is binding on all inferior courts. The doctrine is intended to eliminate vaguer concepts such as justice, fairness, or jurisprudence from influencing decision-making. After all, what do these concepts really mean?

Jurisprudence defies accurate definition, and as a result, it is avoided by the judiciary because of its vagueness. However, it is a concept that is fundamental to understanding English common law, which is the bedrock of our Australian legal system. It is a sort of calibrating mechanism intended to assist the lawyer when confronted with new phenomena. "How should the law address this issue?"

We can get an insight into how this works from a very famous case came before the House of Lords in England in 1932.

A woman went into a café in Scotland with a friend, who bought her a bottle of ginger beer that was in an opaque glass. After she consumed the first glass, she poured the remainder into her glass, and a decomposed snail fell into her glass. The woman was shocked. She suffered gastritis and subsequently, severe nervous shock.

At the time, it was considered to be the law that an action for product defects could only be pursued by the person who purchased the product. In this case, the woman's friend purchased the bottle, which meant that the woman didn't have a remedy for what she suffered.

She must have had a courageous lawyer who decided to sue the manufacturer of the ginger beer. At the trial on the action, she lost. Then she appealed to the House of Lords. One of the Law Lords wouldn't have a bar of her action and held against her. But in a famous moment of judicial history, another Law Lord, Lord Atkin, expressed the view that English jurisprudence must provide a remedy unfettered by historic concepts of the law. He and another of the Law Lords found that the manufacturer of the ginger beer owed a duty to the world at large to ensure that he did not harm them. From that emerged the current law of negligence.

New social phenomena cannot be addressed in our legal system by the application of precedent. It is like driving a car while looking in the rear-vision mirror.

In any event, the disagreement throughout our legal appeals system and at the level of our High Court calls in question the effectiveness of the doctrine of precedent. The rape of a wife in 1674 is a different kettle of fish from the rape of a wife in the twentieth and twenty-first centuries. And yet, in 2004 the High Court revisited the legal scene as it was said to stand in 1674 to determine whether it was still the law in 1963. Three judges said it was no longer the law; two said it was. A touch of jurisprudence would not have gone astray but didn't enter into consideration.

And so we have the emergence of the Aboriginal narrative in the second half of the last century that is constantly being enriched. When the indigenous people have become supplicants to our legal system, its reaction to this new social phenomena is to gaze in the rear-vision mirror of the law. There is no precedent in our law for what was done to the Aboriginal people of this country. Our courts have looked ad nauseam at decisions of courts in America in relation to the Indian population, at decisions in relation to the Inuit people of Canada, the Māori people of New Zealand, and the barbarians and savages of Africa as if they will find some principle of law that preceded the establishment of the outposts of the British Empire. While there is one thing in common—that these people have all been deprived of their heritage by the ascendancy of the British Empire—their stories and circumstances are profoundly different.

The indigenous experiences, in particular the Aboriginal experience, are unique to this country and its historical narrative. As we have seen, the true story of the Aboriginal people has only emerged in recent times. Our High Court has been presented by and had the opportunity to respond to the new discoveries of the sad history of an ancient civilisation. In the event, it was the indigenous people who had to learn the language of our law, research our precedents, and become supplicants to our institutions for remedies to the wrongs they suffered as a result of the imposition of sovereignty and the dispossession from their land. There has never been any suggestion of exploring their precedents or their customs or their laws that had prevailed for tens of thousands of years.

These were opportunities to commence a new page in our jurisprudence, and for the law to turn its back on the saddest period in the history of the original inhabitants is a rejection of fundamental principles of jurisprudence.

On the other hand, if the law were truly committed to precedent, there were two precedents in existence at the time of the arrival of the First Fleet they could have considered. Both international law and English common law provided that sovereignty only passed in relation to new territories that were unoccupied. Both precedents have been ignored.

Faced with the new and evolving indigenous narrative and of the calamities visited by the newcomers on those people, our High Court could have listened to Lord Atkin's invocation of jurisprudence to address a contemporary phenomenon. But they elected to selectively follow so-called precedent.

This course led the court to conclude that native title did exist in 1788, but because at that stage King George III was sovereign over this country, he and subsequent monarchs have extinguished most native title as was the right of the Crown as sovereigns over this country and its people.

The claim by the children who were forcibly and permanently taken from their parents, often with horrendous consequences both to them and their parents, had no foundation in the law of precedent, so consequently, there was no remedy in our law.

Precedent persuaded the majority of the High Court to decide that the amendment to the Constitution in 1967 empowering the Parliament to make laws for the Aboriginal people enabled Parliament to make laws depriving the Aboriginal people of their rights.

And finally, the law of precedent enabled the court to prohibit the indigenous people from challenging the validity of sovereignty over this country, thus closing the door to the claim that they never conceded sovereignty to the Crown.

That is a pretty sad commentary on the operation of the doctrine of precedent in our judicial system.

But by far and away the most profound insult to our jurisprudence were the decisions of the court in Mr Coe's and Mr Mabo's cases that these people had no right to challenge sovereignty in our courts. As we have seen, there is no credible authority for such statements, and to the extent that there are precedents, they are all indicative of the right of the indigenous people to challenge the legality of sovereignty.

`1

"Plus Ça Change, Plus C'est la Même Chose"

"The more things change, the more they stay the same" is a quotation from the French author Jean-Baptiste Alphonse Karr. It is an appropriate observation when considering the performance of our High Court and the operation of the Australian legal system.

Even though officially the Aboriginal people of this country didn't exist according to the constitutional underpinning of sovereignty and dispossession by the Crown, their existence as subjects of British law was established early in the peace. Within fifty years of the arrival of the First Fleet, the newcomers were hanging Aborigines for breaches of British law. Though according to the Constitution the Aboriginal people did not exist, but as people who intersected with the laws of this country, they found themselves imprisoned, shackled, and hanged.

Since those days, there have been the occasional disturbance of Western conscience with a timid amendment to our Constitution in 1967, an "apology" in Parliament in 2004, and a growing awareness of the culture that has been so catastrophically damaged over the past 250 years. But Aborigines are still being imprisoned in numbers that are grotesquely disproportionate to their percentage of the population. They are still dying in custody despite so-called inquiries into the phenomenon.

Our legal system has adjusted to the aberration of disproportionate lawbreaking by the indigenous community. Life expectancy of Aborigines and Torres Straight Islanders is ten years less than white Australians.

There is currently talk of giving the indigenous people a voice. But the fact is that despite everything, nothing has really changed over the past 250 years. Royal commissions, recommendations, inquiries, and money have had the most modest results. All these constructions of our Western society are merely barricades to isolate the main issue, which needs to be resolved if we are to move forward with the indigenous people.

We have to face the fact that the proclamation of sovereignty and the miraculous transfer of ownership of the land are merely myths supported initially by the most absurd assumptions that barbarians and people of a lower order of society populated the country and could be ignored.

One profound change has occurred in the characterisation of the native that populated the country at the time of Captain Cook and the arrival of the first boat people to this country. At that stage, the proclamation of sovereignty and the taking possession of the land of this country were justified by an interpretation of international and English common law at the time. Sovereignty and possession could only pass to a new sovereign in relation to new territory if it was unoccupied. Faced with the fact that this country was occupied by a countless number of natives, the Privy Council dismissed the natives as barbarous, uncivilised, and lacking any system of government that would quality them as people capable of comprehending a civilised system of law. As a result, the country was unoccupied.

But this is where Alphonse Karr's statement is so apposite. It has now emerged and accepted as a legal principle that this country was in fact occupied by the natives in 1788, and the land was not terra nullius. In 1788, the newcomers defended what they were doing on the basis of the law. Today, the same law says that what they did was contrary to the law. Faced with this unanswerable argument that has such serious consequences to our constitutional order, the High Court simply says, "You can't raise that argument in our courts, and that's that."

The more things change, the more they stay the same.

When the reality of indigenous culture was finally revealed to our legal system, the response has been and continues to be a refusal of our High Court to accept that reality. Rather than permitting an open discussion about the legal consequences of the new reality, the court has closed the gate and refused to allow the issue to be argued.

Epilogue

The narrative of the Aboriginal people of this country over the past 250 years is a sad and violent interruption of the process of the previous 60,000 thousand years. Across those millenia, the Aboriginal people cared for this country, learned its ways, and understood its mysterious episodes of droughts, floods, and fires. These were all secret messages that formed part of the ongoing enterprise of their lives in the constant womb of nature. They developed their own stories of creation. These stories are quite beautiful if not naïve, but no more naïve than the story of the golden wand that created the earth and its people in seven days or of the great flood that enabled the good people, such as Noah, to escape.

When one stops to think, and looks objectively at what has happened in this country in the last 250 years, it is quite appalling that in such a brief period, we have insisted that the ancient people abandon their tens of thousands of years of existence and become just like us and subject to our laws. To then punish them for disobedience is almost like prosecuting a person for indecent behaviour who has had his clothes taken from him by the police and then been thrown into the street.

The Aboriginal people have been shorn of their spirituality, their religion, and their beliefs. They have been removed from their land, which was sacred. They have been forced to wear our clothes, use Western names, obey English laws, adopt our religions, abandon their language, learn ours, and lose their sense of land. Their antisocial behaviour is constantly illuminated to display their hopelessness, and they end up in our prisons, where too many of them die.

While there has been some recognition over the past seventy years or so of the tragedy of the Australian Aborigine, it is inevitable that over that time, as more and more people arrive on our shores from overseas communities, the real and meaningful understanding of what has happened to this ancient civilisation escapes most people who have come to enjoy the not inconsiderable benefit of our free and democratic society. But as this wave of migration continues, the newcomers enjoy more of the benefits of our society than the Aboriginal people, who lag behind according the life expectancy and freedom.

Answers still have to be found. I feel deep down that part of the answer has to be in adapting our English jurisprudence to the traditions of these ancient people. Many years ago, having lived in and visited the Northern Territory, I wrote this piece, and I still think it is relevant today.

Dreamtime Interrupted

We tend to think that in this advanced stage of our occupation of this country, there has been time enough for this ancient tribe of people to adjust to our wonderful legal system and process of government so that the conduct of the indigenous people can fairly be judged against the precepts of our highly developed British jurisprudence. It is only fifty years since Judge Kriewaldt expressed his concerns to me about the collision of indigenous and British jurisprudence. That is a few seconds in the timeless period in which the

Aborigines had traditionally respected their own laws and customs.

Margaret Kiddle reflected in *Men of Yesterday* about the Aborigines in the Western District pre-invasion: "The landscapes changed, but the changes were so slow and the generations of men so short that to them change was imperceptible." Suddenly, they were expected to adjust to a rate of change so out of character with their experiences that ruinous fault lines emerged that have never been corrected.

Our prisons are disproportionately populated by indigenous wayward victims of a legal system that has only been operating here in Australia (minus the first 50 years of kangaroo courts) for a bit more than 150 years.

Our expectations that indigenous people adapt to our societal values and processes within a fleeting moment of time on the scale of their history is stupefying in its insensitivity. In recent times, there have been some honourable attempts to establish courts for the administration of aboriginal law, but in the end, most of the aborigines charged and convicted today are charged and convicted in accordance with our jurisprudence, not theirs.

We are living in a country in which the indigenous survivors are still linked emotionally, spiritually, and socially to concepts of morality and behaviour that have their origins in the remote past. To expect them to jettison these concepts overnight and meekly submit to our system of laws and government is the height of hubris.

We refuse to confront a cultural divide that will never be crossed simply by saying, "I am sorry." We need to explore new ways of accommodating our jurisprudence to the ageless habits and customs of those who inhabited the land long before us.

Bibliography

Berndt, R.M and Berndt, C.H., *Aboriginal Man in Australia.* Angus and Robertson, 1965.

Dicey, A. V. *Introduction to the Theory of the Constitution,* 8th edition. Indianapolis: MacMillan, 2015.

Ellis, Jean, comp., with Aboriginal support. *The Dreaming of Aboriginal Australia.* Penrith Art Printing Works, 2006.

Ellis, Jean A. *From the Dreaming.* Harper Collins, 1998.

Flood, Josephine. *The Original Australians.* Allen and Unwin, 2019.

Keay, John. *The Honourable Company.* Harper Collins, 1993.

Neal, Robbi. *Before Time.* Harper Collins, 2016.

Pascoe, Bruce. *Dark Emu.* Magabala Books Aboriginal Corporation, 2018.

Peasley, W. J. *The Last of the Nomads.* Fremantle Press.

Quick and Garren. *The Annotated Constitution of the Australian Commonwealth.* (Facsimile of the 1901 edition.)

Reynolds, Henry. *Dispossession.* Henry Reynolds. Allen and Unwin, 1989.

Strehlow, T. G. H. *Songs of Central Australia.* Angus and Robertson, 1971

Tawney, R. H. *Religions and the Rise of Capitalism.* Maple Press, 2015.

Tyson, Unkaporta. *Sand Talk.* Text Publishing, 2019.

Williams, Brennan, and Lynch. *Australian Constitutional Law and Theory,* 6th edition. Federation Press, 2014.